## What readers are saying

*"A wealth of information!  A must for the small investor..."* (Phyllis Durr, Washington, DC)

*"For the first time in many years I feel like I understand the stock market and the right way to go about investing."* (Tom Kay, Houston, TX)

*"I must say that both the class and the book are one of the best investments I have made already."* (Bruce Hop, Austin, TX)

*"Highly recommended."* (Wisconsin Bookwatch)

*"I've taken many classes over the years and, I must say, yours was the best..."* (Sandy Stout, Oceanside, CA)

*"Thanks for all the great information!  I am so fired up!"* (Lisha Rigney, Los Angeles, CA)

*"...so simple it's actually enjoyable...investing really is for everyone..."* (Manny Carbahal, CPA, Davis, CA)

*"...inspiring..."* (Pamela Hull, Financial Manager, Los Angeles, CA)

**W9-ANF-310**

# BUILDING YOUR FINANCIAL PORTFOLIO
## ON $25 A MONTH (OR LESS)
© 2000

Bobbie Christensen
Eric Christensen

**EFFECTIVE LIVING PUBLISHING**
P. O. Box 232233
Sacramento, CA 95823
ELPBooks@aol.com

Published by Effective Living Publishing
P.O.Box 232233, Sacramento, CA 95823
(916) 422-8435; orders (800) 929-7889
Email: ELPBooks@aol.com
Website: www.BooksAmerica.com

# TABLE OF CONTENTS

Why Should I Invest My Paycheck When I Can Barely
Make Ends Meet? What Can I Do With Only $25 A
Month? Where Can I Invest My Money Safely?
Everyone Who Has Played "Monopoly" Knows It
Takes Money To Make Money; Can I Be Successful
Without A Big Bankroll?

So What Can I AFFORD To Invest In? Savings
Account; Certificates of Deposit; Real Estate, Gold,
and Collectibles; Mutual Funds; Investment Clubs;
IRA's and Employee Pension Plans; Stocks

After Paying The Bills, How Can I Invest In Anything?

Now That I've Got A Little Stash, What Do I Do With
It? Gut Instinct; Research; Reinvestment; Splits

## INTRODUCTION

Welcome to the world of investing! We say welcome because this book is meant for the beginning investor or the person who wants to find a safe, secure place to put their money, where it will grow 100% or more a year, but without having to spend a lot of time doing the research or worrying about their investments. You will also learn very important information on how to cut out stock broker fees and expenses thus keeping that money in your own pocket. We feel it is important for everyone to take charge of their own lives and their own finances rather than put $1,000 of your hard-earned money into an over-diversified mutual fund that will grow no more than 30% a year and at considerable risk.

You will find all of the necessary steps, carefully outlined and in detail, to find these safe companies as well as how to actually do the investing. We feel everyone in this country should have access to this important information without having to pay hundreds of dollars for books, tapes, or seminars. We are not brokers and have no vested interest in any company mentioned in this book. Our purpose is strictly to educate. We are retired bankers and financial managers who have successfully used this method of investing for ourselves over the last 20 years as well as taught it to thousands of others

Afterall, we all know we need to save, both for our own well-being and for the well-being of our country's economy. Too often, however, we are lead to believe that we need to be rich (or at least have $1,000) in order to invest our money. No you don't! To make this information available to everyone, this book is specifically written to be easily understood by anyone from 13 years old to 90. After you have started your investment plan, share this with your children and grandchildren or, if you are a teacher, with your students.

The point of this book is to show you how to use just $25 (or less) a month to build your portfolio. But remember, $25 is a random amount we have chosen; you can use this same method of investing using less money or a great deal more. Keep in mind that this book is for people who want to invest SAFELY but with tremendous GROWTH. Because you will be using a safe method, fluctuations in the stock market will not effect your investment and you will be able to sleep nights without worrying.

This book is also for the person who does not find numbers or the stock market all interesting and, thus, does not want to spend a lot of time on research. It takes a lot of time to invest in high-risk stock because you have to be constantly watching the market and making buying and selling decisions. With low-risk long-term investments, you make your decision choosing only from the safe investments and do not have to look at it again until you need to retrieve some money. If you find this book very interesting and would like to learn more about investing, see the flyer in the back of this book on the sequel, *Adding To Your Financial Portfolio.* There is also information on our newest books including *Top 50 Best Stock Investments* to save you time.

Please note that this is the 3rd edition of this book. The 1st edition of *Building Your Financial Portfolio On $25 A Month (Or Less)* won the 1998 Best Business Book of the Year Award and became a best-seller. The 2nd edition sold even better. After selling hundreds of thousands of these editions, we felt it was time to add new information to keep you informed of what is happening in the stock market and to your money. And, yes, we have included more stories.

Many people have helped with this book and supported our endeavors. Among them are Manny Carbohol, CPA; Bess Chen, Loren Kammerer and the whole staff of the Martin Luther King Branch Library who helped with the research; Bob Scott, a friend and mathematician who understands numbers and formulas better than we do; Barbara Scott for her unflagging encouragement; our many seminar participants who showed us what they want and need to know; and our patient and self-reliant children, Anna and David. And to all of you who will, by using this information, help us fulfill our obligation to make a difference in this world.

Please use this method to build your own financial security and remember to have fun watching your money grow.

Bobbie & Eric Christensen
Sacramento, CA
January 2000

# I. WHO CAN INVEST IN WHAT; AND WHEN, WHY, AND HOW SHOULD I INVEST?

## Why Should I Invest My Paycheck When I Can Barely Make Ends Meet?

We all should!  And that means anyone from 10 years old to 65 or even older.  We have all heard this a thousand times.  Even if our parents did not tell us, we would have heard it on a newscast or some talk show.  So we all know how important it is to save for the future, but how many of us are actually doing something about it?  How many are just procrastinating and then one day, or more specifically on our 60th birthday, realize we have put it off for too long.

And what is the major reason for putting off saving, besides procrastination?  It is the same reason we put off most things in life - - money and knowledge.  We tell ourselves that we just do not have anything extra to invest right now, but we will some day. Some day has come! Or we feel we do not know how to invest and must, therefore, go to a stock broker (and pay their fees and monthly expenses) and get trapped in a mutual fund that will grow, at best, 30% a year. Any average intelligent person (or teenager) can understand the market **if it is explained to them**. We are here to explain it to you and tell what no broker will ever tell you.

Recently some of our schools have started teaching our children about investing for the future. Some (unfortunately not many) students in this country, from high school through college, have had fun playing investment games where they pretend to pick and buy stocks and then watch what happens. In the standard classroom setting, students are given $100,000 (just pretend money) to invest in the stock market. This is an excellent educational tool to help teach our children about one aspect of our economy. Wouldn't it be even more fun to use real money to teach your children how to invest safely? Obviously, we are not going to give them $100,000, nor should we. The problem with the method being used in our schools is that it teaches our children that the only way you can invest in the market is if you already have a great deal of money sitting around. Just recently on our local news, a school using this program was highlighted. The interesting thing about this news segment was that, after taking this program, most of the students said that when they were out of school and had a high paying job, they would invest in the stock market. Only two students understood that they could invest without having a huge amount of money.

By giving anyone this much money in order to learn about the market, you are telling them that they **must** have this much money in order to be able to invest. This is just simply not true. However, if your intention is to discourage them from ever investing in their own future, you will do an excellent job of it.

What we should be teaching students, and everyone else in this country, is that the stock market is an opportunity we are all given no matter how much, or little, money you have. It is a way to make money that is open to everyone regardless of sex, religion, race, or anything else! If a teenager is working and earning some money each week, they should follow the directions given here and watch their own money grow. And, if they do **not** follow these directions for **safely** investing their money but decide instead to choose risky investments, they will learn quickly why that is not a good idea and yet only risk loosing $100 or less. We think nothing of putting checks we are given at our babies birth into a savings account for them. Afterall, we want to save for our baby's future. But why not put it into an investment that will be safe and yet will have a great deal more growth potential then a little savings account making 2% interest.

The same is true for adults. It is safe to say that most people do not understand how the stock market works and, therefore, have developed the opinion that only the very rich segment of our population can earn "free" money in the stock market as well as other investment areas. We hear of someone buying $100,000 worth of stock and having it become $1,000,000 seemingly overnight. But, the majority of our populace does not have $100,000 to invest. The majority do not even have the $1,000 minimum necessary to invest in a mutual fund. Certainly not when they are in their twenties and just starting out in life. Yet this is the time that they should be saving for their first home or for retirement. After all, the government starts taking social security out of our pay checks immediately, so why shouldn't we take something out for our own financial future?

Of course, a regular savings account is an investment and you can put in just pennies if you want to, but it can be terribly boring watching your $10 grow by $.02 a month. With our investment plan you can watch it grow up to 100% a year or even more, plus have the excitement of seeing a 3 for 1 split triple your investment "overnight". We will even show how an initial investment of just one share of stock and $25 a month can become $100,000 or more in just 10 years. With our method you will be doing a little bit more than putting money into a savings account but earning a lot more.

By the way, this is not some new method that we came up with. If you had read The Wall Street Journal every day for five years, you would already know about this. But most of our population is not interested and, therefore, does not read financial information. We have simply taken the information that is out there and put it into book (and seminar) form because a broker wants to control your money with a mutual fund so that he can make his living. It is your choice where to invest your money, but we feel it is only fair that you have all the facts first.

Investing in the stock market, whether on your own or through an investment club or by way of mutual funds, is a legalized form of gambling. Or perhaps you had parents like mine that taught you that everything in life is a gamble. You are gambling when you start a new job, get married, buy a house, and at many other times in your life. But we do not think of it as gambling because we feel we are investing in our future. When we marry, we know there is the possibility (and a very great possibility today) that it will not work out. Yet most of us will take that risk. Certainly one of the biggest risks we can take with our financial security is starting our own business, but thousands of people are doing just that every year, now more than ever. Most people, even kids, find a certain pride in having their lemonade stand, selling their extra produce, having a part-time consulting business, opening a computer training center, or any of the thousands of other choices in life. Having a small part-time business usually does not pose any threat to your financial well-being. But renting space, leasing equipment, hiring help, and opening a computer training center could be a threat.

Investing your money should actually be much safer then starting your own business. Yet the majority of new small businesses fail within the first five years. Why? Because they had not researched the market enough, they did not know how to market themselves, they did not have enough financial backing, etc., etc. When you invest in the stock market, you are investing in a company and becoming a part owner of it. Therefore, you need to do the same things you would do in starting your own business. That is, you need to research and find out if they know how to market themselves, if they have financial backing, if they are succeeding. In this book, we are going to explain how to do this research using just a few minutes of your time and, who knows, maybe you will learn things that will help you start your own successful business.

There is always the possibility of losing money when you invest it. However, by following our method, you will create minimum risk for your money with maximum gain!

Learning about the financial world and enjoying the excitement of this legal form of gambling are only very small parts of why you should be investing. The important reason for doing this is for YOU. Are there things you want in life but feel you will never be able to afford? Are you worried about your future and how you will survive when you retire? Are you in the majority of working people who cannot afford life insurance and, therefore, worry about your family if something should happen to you? Do you just want more out of your life?

Probably most people think at one time or another of owning their own business and, for one reason or another, never get around to doing it. Investing in the stock market is investing in a company and becoming part owner of it. You may feel that you do not have enough money to start your own business, but you have enough to invest in another business and take pride in watching that company grow and prosper and taking you right along with it.

# What Can I Do With Only $25 A Month?

Anyone can use this method for investing whether you are on a very small budget or have thousands of dollars to invest. You will all follow the same steps. But for our examples, we are going to assume you only have $25 a month that you can put away keeping in mind that it can also be done on as little as $10 a month.

So what can you do with only $25 a month? How about buy your first home or a new, larger home? Or get a college degree? Or even be able to retire early? If you are trying to save for your first home, you may be wondering whether owning a house is worth it if you have to save for twenty years just to get a minimum down payment. That in itself is a major problem because the smaller your down payment, the higher your monthly payment will be which will put even more stress on your small budget. Also, in today's market place, we all need to wonder whether investing in our own house is a good investment or will the value decrease below it's purchase price as has been happening in many areas of the country (you might want to take a look at *Building Your Debt Free Life*. But it does seem to be a natural instinct to want a place of our own. So do you think it would help if you could save all of the down payment you will need in 5 years instead of 10 years?

When you are in your twenties, you probably do not want to be tied down to a house and its payments, yet that is a good time to be saving for it. You might be reading this right now and saying to yourself, "I'm only 21 years old and plan on enjoying my freedom for quite awhile before settling down with a spouse, kids, and a house!" But even at 21 you can probably think of other things you would like to do. How about that trip around the world before you settle down or that Porsche. Or how about retiring at an early age.

The point is, you can and should invest in your future even if you do not have a clear goal. But it is certainly a lot more difficult when you do not have a goal. It is a fact that it is almost impossible to accomplish anything in life if you have not already figured out what it is you want. So if you have to, just invent something in your mind that you want to save for. After all, there is no law against changing your mind in the future when you have enough money from your investments to do whatever you want to do. But it is important in anything, whether career, family life, or your personal life, to have goals you are headed toward. If you need help with figuring out "what you want to be when you grow up", read my first book, *Getting A Free Education: The Key To Your Dream Job*.

If you are in your thirties, do you want to go back to school or do you want to help your children go to college some day? You can actually start your children on saving the day they are born with just a few dollars a month.

You could put that few dollars into a bank savings account at 2% interest but wouldn't it be more effective to put it into a safe long-term investment that is earning an average of 50% to 100% a year. Then when he or she is old enough to work part-time, they can be adding to their investments every month. The same goes for your own education. Just because you cannot afford to go to college directly out of high school does not mean life is over. You can still have a wonderful career or start your own business, you can still marry and raise a wonderful and happy family without college. But if you start saving from every paycheck as soon as you get out of high school, you will be surprised at how quickly those few dollars can grow.

Do you want to live comfortably when you retire and/or be able to retire before age 65? That is probably the number one financial concern of people in their forties and upward. We know that the social security system was created as something to help the older citizen survive retirement. It is important to remember that it was never meant to be the sole support of anyone. Therefore, it is up to each of us to take care of our own futures. Currently, 4.5% of your pay check goes into the social security system. If you make only $5 an hour, that is about $9 a week or $36 a month. Could you afford to save that much each month for your own use? Can you afford to save just 1% or $8 a month? Also, be aware that some legislators in Washington would like to have a percentage of our social security withholding put into an investment of your choice. Unfortunately, the "choice" they want is between different mutual funds where you will have more risk and lower growth then you will from making your individual investments.

You see, it does not take much to invest in yourself and, when you make your own investments, you are controlling it and do not have to worry about politicians using your money for something else or about it going bankrupt and you loosing all of your money. Then, if social security is still around when you retire, it will be what it was meant to be: an additional help in your retirement years, not your sole support. Let your government-controlled social security grow little by little but have your own investments grow 100% or more a year.

The point is, investing is a way to save for short-term as well as long-term things while remembering that short-term investing is riskier with more of a chance of losing money (we will discuss this in chapter IV). A pension plan is a long-term investment because it is meant only for your retirement with a sizable penalty if you withdraw **your** money early. And remember that even with a pension plan, we are talking about **your** money, not someone else's. When we talk about saving using our method for long-term things such as a downpayment on a home, we are talking about 10 years (give or take a couple of years). That may sound like a very long time to you but, compared to a pension plan, it is very short time. Also, investing for the long-term or at least 10 years will tie you into certain investing fundamentals to insure higher safety. We will discuss these later.

Social scientists say we are living in a time when people have come to expect "instant gratification". Well, those social scientists know that there is no such thing as instant gratification - - everything takes time. You and I know that, too. However, even after we lecture you on not expecting instant gratification, it is very satisfying to have your own savings system in place whereby you can watch your money growing on a monthly basis and know that you are the one doing it. It may not be instant, but it is filled with gratification. And you will have only yourself to praise for doing it and, believe it or not, you can actually have fun saving. After all, if you have a hobby of collecting something, say Christmas tree ornaments, it is fun seeing a new one added to your collection. Seeing your money increase in an easy and painless fashion can be just as satisfying. Every time your stock splits and you have new shares that you didn't even have to pay for, you will have a tangible item to add to your investing "collection". Maybe we should get rid of the word "saving" and instead call it "collecting"!

Should you invest to get rich? "The man who starts out simply with the idea of getting rich won't succeed; you must have a larger ambition." (John D. Rockefeller) The idea of Scrooge hoarding his pence is funny to us, but that is what happens when we invest just to become rich. Investing for your future is a much better ambition. And we would be willing to bet that if we asked you what you would like to do when you retire if money were no object, you could probably come up with some very interesting pursuits, and not one of those pursuits would be sitting all alone in a vault counting your money.

There was an interesting story we once heard about a typical couple who retired. He had worked hard at a blue-collar job all of his life. His wife had stayed home to raise the children and take care of their home. They had to pinch pennies, but they were happy. Then, when he retired at 65, his wife told him they had won a contest and the prize was a beautiful cruise to Hawaii. They had a wonderful trip, but he was spending a great deal of time worrying about how they would survive now that he was retired. She finally told him that he did not have to worry any more, that they had not won the cruise, but that she had been saving just a few dollars each week out of the grocery money and investing it in the stock market. Now they were quite wealthy and he would not have to worry any more. Needless to say, he was very surprised but very happy.

Unlike some of the infomercials you see on TV, we are not talking about getting rich. We are talking about putting your money into secure investments that will provide you with a comfortable living realizing that "comfortable" can mean different things to different people. We are talking about security for your hard earned pay check. However, likewise, we cannot promise that you will not become rich. For some people, having investments worth $100,000 is rich while to others nothing short of a billion dollars is rich. Also, becoming "comfortable" or "rich" depends on whether you follow our method so as not to lose the money you have saved and whether you follow our steps and thus increase your savings each month. It also depends on when you actually *start* investing.

We realize that it is easier to read this book and say you are going to do it then it is to actually start doing it. If you begin saving when you are 50 years old, you will not be able to build up quite as much as you would if you started at 30. Likewise, by starting as teenagers at 13 years old, they will not only be assured of having a comfortable retirement but, in all probability, will be able to retire at a much younger age.

What we can promise you is that our method provides a safe way to increase your savings at a much faster rate than your savings account or mutual fund ever will.

18

## Where Can I Invest My Money Safely?

There are many investments to choose from including stocks, bonds, Certificates of Deposit, treasury notes, real estate, mutual funds, and others. However, this book is devoted to investing SAFELY but with much better growth then any of these other vehicles can provide. In chapter IV, we will be talking about all of these choices and each of their pros and cons, but our method uses only one possible investment. And what do we consider a safe place to put our money?

The stock market. The stock market?! Safe?! Are you kidding?! No, we are not kidding. Before we get into a brief description of all of the other options, let's see why the stock market can provide you with the best return in the safest manner so you will have something to compare the others to.

First, keep in mind that the stock market has out-performed all of the other forms of investment since the turn of the century (yes, including the crash of 1929). Since 1929, the stock market has increased in value 3 out of every 5 years. Unfortunately, due to the inability of others to invest wisely, too many people feel that the stock market is gambling. It is not gambling if you are investing in safe companies to begin with. For instance, we were all taught in history class about the Great Crash of October 1929 and how it lead to a severe worldwide depression that lasted for 10 years and we only came out of because of World War II. However, the numbers say something else. Yes, the entire stock market dropped drastically from 1929 through 1932. But after that the Dow Jones Industrial Average zoomed right back up. Why is this different from our history classes?

First, understand that the Dow Jones Industrial Average (the closing figure you here on the news each day) is made up of the most important industries in our country and the top 30 companies from those industries. When the crash occurred, these strong 30 companies did not close their doors or even layoff workers. Instead, they waited out the initial public panic and then proceeded to prosper through the rest of the thirties. These are the kind of strong investments we are looking for (see *Top 50 Best Stock Investments*).

Second, remember that there are steps to follow in order to invest safely that we will be covering later. If you decide not to follow these steps and start investing in riskier stocks with the hope of a faster growth, you will be risking your own future. If you are looking to become rich overnight and invest in those stocks that have a vague chance of increasing dramatically in an extremely short time period, you are risking losing your money dramatically and extremely quickly. And the risk of that happening if you do not follow this method is extremely high.   Historically, the individual investor who sticks with safe investments has always made more money then stock brokers have.   However, this makes sense since we probably care more about our money then any stock broker that makes his living off of our money.

The third reason to invest in the stock market is that it is the one we can all afford.  As the title of this books says, you can invest $25 or less every month and then sit back and watch your investment grow.   You might think that joining a mutual fund or an investment club is the same thing but it is not.  These both require a good deal more than $25 to start with (usually a minimum of $1,000) without the safety or huge growth.

The fourth reason is actually a number of good reasons:  the stock market allows you to choose your own investments thus giving you complete control of your money, you can actually become part owner of a company which means partaking of certain perks, and it is fun.

Investing in the stock market is legalized gambling.   If you are already addicted to gambling, do not get into the market until you get medical help.   Gambling addiction is a compulsive illness that can be overcome.   To invest wisely, you MUST invest with your head, not your heart.   Occasionally you can invest using both your head and your heart, but not very often. The co-author of this book once decided, against the advice of her husband and co-author, to invest a few dollars in a new company started by a famous actor that she was very fond of. She purchased 10 shares at $17 the day this new company went public on the stock exchange. This stock has never seen $17 since that day. Fortunately, she has not lost this money because she has not sold it yet - - she cannot afford to sell it! But she now understands about using your head rather than your heart when you invest in anything. However, we will now contradict ourselves.

Occasionally you can invest using your head AND your heart as when we invested in Disney. Its long term history is excellent (so our heads were satisfied) even if we did spend our honeymoon at Disney World (our hearts told us to do it). Actually, this demonstrates one of the best reasons for investing in any company and that is **invest in companies that you know and understand and use**. Besides being very familiar with the Disney movies, we knew their parks (we visit every year), how they are kept neat and clean, the great attitude of their employees, etc. If we had gone to a park and found it dirty and in disrepair, we doubt that our hearts would have said "this is the one".

In the following chapters, you will learn how to develop your own investment plan that will give you a road map to carefully follow and to keep your emotions in check. Just like a road map, if you do not follow your financial plan, it will take you longer and cost you more to get where you want to go, if you get there at all. Developing a plan probably sounds very much like getting organized. Well, it is necessary to become at least a little organized. For some of you, that means "oh no, I can't do this, I'm totally unorganized". Don't panic. We have written our method down in book form and in detail just to help you. You will have all the steps carefully numbered so you won't forget anything.

Besides giving you the details of what to invest in and how to invest, we will be helping you with other areas directly connected to your financial plan. To develop your plan, you will need to decide how much you can invest and where to invest it. Also, if you learn here how to **write down** your plans, you will find that having everything in black and white will keep you from making serious mistakes. In fact, if you can learn to create written plans to continually read and follow, you will avoid making mistakes in all areas of your life.

Remember also that if you keep in mind that you are investing for the long term or what you will have after 5, 10, 20, or 30 years, you will be less likely to make mistakes caused by greed or fear. Greed can lead you to make investment purchases trying to become instantly rich and fear can make you sell a safe investment and, thus, lose future earnings you would have had. We all must take chances in life, but we must learn how to take carefully researched chances that we know, in all probability, will succeed.

You may work for someone else right now but, when it comes to investing your money, you are working for yourself and you are the boss. As such, you must learn not to make decisions based on your fear of what the market might do tomorrow (no one can truly predict this). It is not actually "fear" anyway. What most people feel that keeps them from accomplishing so much in their lives is a small nagging doubt. People who are constantly buying and selling are either trying a false way of getting rich quick (that is to buy low and sell high over and over again) or they are letting their doubts and emotions make their decisions. If you invest in companies that meet our safety criteria, your stock will still have ups and downs but will quickly regain whatever you might have lost during a brief downturn or even during a longer recession if you hold on to it and don't panic. For instance, Coca-Cola stock dropped just like everyone else in the 1929 crash. Yet, within 18 months it was selling at the same price as the day before the crash started. Do not waste your time watching the stock market every day trying to decide if you should sell this stock and buy that stock. Relax and enjoy the cozy feeling of knowing that your money is safe.

Certainly you can buy stock when it costs the least amount and sell it when it is at it's highest amount but that is what we cover in our book for intermediate investors, *Adding To Your Financial Portfolio,* who are willing to spend time every day on their portfolio. The point we are trying to make is that you can be investing a little each month in a safe company and still be following the rule "buy low and sell high". We will explain that later. Buying and selling every day is not fun and will just keep you from getting a good night's sleep. Historically, these "day traders" do not make any money simply because their broker fees eat up any profit.

We will be investing in stocks considered to be in the blue-chip category, that is, in large, healthy, growing companies that will still be around when your grandchildren are investing. Please do not confuse OUR blue-chip list with the blue chip list the New York Stock Exchange considers "blue chip". It takes the market a long time, sometimes years, to catch up with what is actually happening in the stock market. Therefore, stocks that are extremely stable can take years or even decades to become an actual Blue Chip Stock even though they have already reached that status in the real world. You will be developing your own list of blue chip stocks based on your own sound yet easy research.

Always remember that when you buy stock in a business, you are buying a part of that company. So, do you want to buy a get-rich-quick dream or a solid American business? Yes, we have all heard of the entrepreneurs who buy into a small company and then one year later sell their stock at a profit to "get rich". You have to decide for yourself what kind of person you are. Do you really want to gamble your whole future everyday on such a risky investment? Psychologists tell us that security is an ingrown need after food and shelter. Therefore, we are assuming in this book that the vast majority of people want security. We personally want security for our own money. Thus, our method of investing is based on safety for our money and yours.

Generally speaking, the smaller the company is, the riskier the stock is. Also, any stock that sells at $10.00 or less is usually remarkably risky. Historically, the odds are extremely high that company will not make it.

You may have wished that you had invested in some of the technology stocks when they first came out but, when they first became public, no one had any way of knowing which ones would succeed and which ones would fail and the people investing in them were the owners and employees. And the vast majority of the technology stocks have not done well even though we remember only the ones that have changed the world, so to speak. 9 out of every 10 new businesses fail within the first five years. You could have bought one share of Intel when they went public in 1971 for $23. Today that one share has multiplied and is worth over $900,000. Remember that it does no good to worry about the one that got away. You will do best to think about what the future of that successful technology firm will be. For several years it seemed that MicroSoft could do no wrong, but what will be the result of the government lawsuit against them, and what about 10 years from now. There was a time when Apple Computer could do no wrong but things changed. If there is a world-wide catastrophe such as a financial collapse or even natural disasters, will technology be considered a basic necessity of life? When natural or man-made disasters occur, we know that people are concerned with rebuilding their homes, finding grocery stores that are open and have food and water to buy. After a hurricane, flood, tornado, etc., schools are concerned with rebuilding and getting the basic supplies, not buying new computers. A business that has been physically ruined will be back in business quickly if they supply a necessity of life rather than the unnecessary things. We will be discussing the difference between the necessities of life that people will always need and the other things in life that come and go depending on the situation later in this book.

It is always fun to play the "what if I had invested in MicroSoft the first day it was issued" game. But that is a very chancy game to play with real money. Doesn't this just prove that the stock market is too risky? Not at all. We will be showing you how to find the success stories that you will not have to worry about. And we are not bashing MicroSoft but only pointing out something that all technology companies already know or should know. That is, until the day arrives that we literally cannot survive, live and not die, without technology, it is not truly necessary. So long as we can shelter ourselves and grow food and find clean water without technology, it is not necessary. But it certainly does make life a lot easier and more pleasant! Remember that we have invested in Disney stock and that is certainly not a necessity of life. We will be talking more about investing in the necessary stocks first and the unnecessary ones second as our portfolio grows.

Remember that one of our primary goals is to invest our money where it will grow to give us more wealth. According to numbers compiled for the Standard & Poor 500, it has shown a 9% return during the last 25 years, out-performing corporate bonds (4.4%), treasury bills (3.3%), and inflation (3.3%). Of course, the stock market has drops that can effect the day to day value of your portfolio but, in the last 50 years, the safe secure stocks that have dropped have regained their original value in no more than 24 months. That means that to invest safely in the market, you must invest for the long haul so that you will not have to worry about how a recession or brief drop is affecting your portfolio.

Plus, you actually save money by not constantly buying and selling.

The obvious savings is in knowing that stock brokers charge for every purchase and sale or transaction. A transaction is the buying or selling of stock in a particular company. Thus if you buy stock in two different companies, that is two transactions. Even using our method, you may be paying a one-time broker fee for an initial purchase or subsequent sale. Therefore, you want to be very sure that the stock you are holding is going to drop in price and continue to drop before you decide to sell it and, using our method, you should end up with stocks so strong that their value will always rise again.

Remember that one of our points is to make investing fun and something you do not need to be an expert in. If you have to watch your portfolio every day to decide whether to buy or sell, you will not be having fun. Also note that watching the stock market every day can drive a normal person to insanity! Of course, there are those people who do consider that fun, but we are writing for the average citizen, just like us, who considers traveling, snorkeling, hiking, going to the theater and such as a lot more fun then sitting home every day because we have to keep an eye on our investments and not sleeping at night worrying whether we should have sold that day. Our method is only for the person who does not want to become an expert in investing.

It is a fact that most ordinary citizens have consistently made better market decisions then the professional analysts and brokers have. In 1995 the Beardstown Ladies ' became quite famous for their book *The Beardstown Ladies' Common-Sense Investment Guide*. Because they had higher growth on their stock picks then any broker in the country, their book became a best-seller. Since then they have written other books and had extensive media coverage. However, a couple of years ago it came out in the news that there had been an error and their portfolio had not had the best growth (although they had still done better than most brokers). This discovery proved very embarrassing and they looked into what they had done wrong. They found that they had based their figures on the dollar amount they had invested and what it was now worth. However, they had forgotten to include their broker fees and monthly expenses for handling their account for them. If they had invested using our method, they would not have had those expenses and would still be beating all of the brokers. The point is, you can make wise decisions and keep your money in your own pocket.

Even the best educated analysts and brokers are just people and they do make mistakes. Then, to double their mistakes, they insist on buying and selling continually. If you feel you must deal with these people, NEVER follow their advice without first checking the stock yourself using our step-by-step method in chapter IV.  Many years ago, the co-author worked for a large stock brokerage firm in Boston.  It seemed amazing to her at the time that, even when the broker invested unwisely and a person lost not only what dividends had been earned but even lost their initial investment, that person still had to pay the broker's fee every month.  In other words, the broker makes his money whether he makes a good decision for you or not.  Please consider that brokers only make that fee when they buy or sell a stock for you; thus, you will find that the stocks in any one mutual fund will be continually changing.

If you think that you need a Ph.D. in order to invest your own money, let me ask you how many rich Ph.D.'s do you know?  Besides, as Ben Franklin the creator of the first public library knew, you can learn anything you want or need to know at your library.  In fact, virtually all of the research we will be talking about can be done for free at the library.  Even if you find yourself enjoying the complexities of the stock market and want to become an expert in it, you can get all the advice and knowledge of the very best experts from the books those experts have written at your library.  You never need to depend on just your local broker's opinion.

For that matter, do not completely depend on and trust anyone else's opinion.  You would be amazed at how many of your friends and relatives will be more then willing to offer their advice on investing your money. You should certainly listen to these people and gather all the information you can but, as you listen, you must consider whether they actually know what they are talking about. You may have a sister who works as a bank teller, but that does not make her an expert on banking; however, you need to consider whether she has done extensive research on the banking industry and what outside places she is getting her facts from. In all probability, if she is repeating what her boss has told her concerning how safe an investment in her bank is, you are hearing the morale boosters that all of the employees hear. But, if she is quoting The Wall Street Journal, you may want to follow up her research with your own to see if this particular bank is a good investment.

It is not necessary to be an expert with a complicated system to succeed in the stock market. You will find that our method is very simple and takes very little time. You can spend as little as hour a month on your investing or, if you find it more interesting than you thought it would be, you can spend lots of time on it. Stock brokers are considered experts in the field but there are not many rich ones; if they are rich, why do they still work so hard to get your fees? And the stock market itself is not that complicated to understand. If you want to start a company and need cash to buy a building and supplies, then you look for investors. Once you have that business established and want to expand your company, you again look for investors. That is what the stock market is. The system of buying and selling on the floor of the New York Stock Exchange is very confusing, almost seeming to verge on mayhem. But only a brokerage firm that has bought a seat on the floor of the stock exchange can be on that floor so you do not need to worry about all of that mayhem. However, if you are going to be in New York, the stock exchange does give very interesting tours.

Nevertheless, it is a certain fact that no one is more interested in your money then you are! Well, with the possible exception of Uncle Sam and, as you get older, your children. You have worked hard to earn your money and you should be the one making decisions on how to invest your money. Trusting someone else to do what is best for you is never a good idea and definitely not a good idea when it comes to your future survival and comfort.

To answer the original question, what should you invest in in order to have safe low-cost high-growth investments that you will not have to constantly watch and become an expert in? **You are going to learn how to find the large, well-known, growing companies and then how to save money while using every technique available to increase your investment quickly and safely.**

## Everyone Who Has Played "Monopoly" Knows It Takes Money To Make Money; Can I Be Successful Without A Big Bankroll?

As William J. O'Neil said, "Success in a free country is simple. Get a job, get an education, and learn to save and invest wisely." Hopefully, you already have the job (if not, order "Getting A Free Education: The Key To Your Dream Job" by this author on the form at the end of this book). And everyone should be constantly learning new things. This book will give you the knowledge you need to save your money and invest wisely.

O'Neil also said that in his experience "a person's years and quality of education have very little to do with making big money investing in the market." And he is right - - even children can learn to invest and some of the most successful investors in history never graduated from high school. However, he left out another very important point. It also does not matter whether you are a man or a woman. When it comes to investing our own money, we are all created equal and there is no "glass ceiling" on your potential. Women can invest as wisely as men and you do not need your spouse's permission to invest your own money. And guess what? The opportunities in investing are equal for everyone, regardless of race, religion, or age, too! Our country is supposed to be a free-market society and, when it comes to investing, it really is.

And finally, if you do not ever take the first step toward securing your financial future, you will never reach it. As we always say, if you don't believe you can, then you can't. We know that getting past the little doubts and taking that first step in any endeavor is always the most difficult one, but we hope that this book (and perhaps *Top 50 Best Stock Investments*) will give you an easy plan to follow and will reduce the fears you may have. Only you can take those few dollars to make your first investment. Even if you never invest another dollar, at least you will have done something for your future. But we certainly hope that you will continue to invest. We know that you can do it because if we can, anyone can.

## II. WHAT TO INVEST IN!

### So What Can I AFFORD To Invest In?

Let's talk about some of the different kinds of investments and the pros and cons of each. For each one we will need to keep in mind certain factors such as how much money is required to get started, how safe is it, how fast will it grow. We are only considering some of the most common savings methods so that you can easily compare these systems with the stock market. Knowing that at this point you do not want to use all of your spare time working on your investments, we are not considering the many other savings options that require in-depth knowledge, huge fees, large initial investments, etc. Keep in mind the four reasons we listed for investing in the stock market: **it has outperformed all other forms of investment, it can be very safe if done properly, it is within even a very tight budget, and it allows you to control exactly what happens to your money.** Compare the history of security, ease of use, and the amount of initial investment needed for each of the following with that of the stock market.

## Savings Account

For those who are older in our reading audience, you may remember that there used to be a time when putting your money into a savings account was an excellent investment. When we were children, we never received lower than a 5% return on our savings and sometimes as much as 10%. Now our banks are very profitable to their Boards of Directors but not to the public whose money they use to create that profitability for their owners. Currently, you can only expect about 2% and be prepared to have service charges taken out of your account also. Therefore, you might want to consider investing in stock in the banking industry, but don't think of a savings account as an investment that will secure your future.

Also, keep in mind that with several investment instruments such as savings accounts and Certificates of Deposit, you are actually giving your money to someone to invest in the stock market for you. The difference is that you put your money into a regular savings account and get 2% interest on your money. At the same time, the bank is using your money to invest in several things along with the stock market and getting as much as a 15% or more return and giving you only that 2%. The banks attitude is that they are giving you the privilege of investing with them so that they can give you as little as possible and they can make as high a profit as possible (if we seem prejudiced, remember that we are retired bankers and know what goes on). Instead, why not develop your own attitude of investing where you will get the highest return for your money and always remembering that you are giving the bank the privilege of using your money.

However, having said all of this, we confess that we will be using savings accounts in our method, but in a very limited way. After all, everything has its proper place.


## Certificates of Deposit

We don't think Certificates of Deposit should be called CD's any more due to the possibility of being confused with something that we play and listen to. But for the brevity of this book, they will be called CD's.

A CD is money that you choose to invest in a type of savings account that, because of the high initial investment and the fact that you cannot touch your money for a guaranteed amount of time, will give you a higher rate of return. Many banks have a minimum deposit of $1,000 or more along with a penalty for early withdrawal.  If you have this much extra money sitting around that you can tie up for at least one year, then you might want to look into a CD after carefully checking all of the possible interest rates.   They vary widely but are averaging only 5% return currently.   This is certainly a very safe place to invest your money. However, we are interested in investments that require a much smaller initial sum of money and will actually have a  much higher rate of growth.


## Real Estate, Gold, and Collectibles

Real estate can be very lucrative, but you can also quite literally lose your shirt in it. Whether or not real estate is a good investment is very dependent on the economic situation of the country and even the specific area of the country you are interested in at the time, and that situation can change very quickly.   With today's housing market, even owning your own home is not necessarily as good an investment as it used to be (see *Building Your Debt Free Life)*.  Nationwide recessions have taught us that the value of the house you buy can easily drop below what you paid for it and it can take as long as 10 years to get that value back, if ever.

Of course, the value of any investment, including the stock market, can also change very quickly.  However, our major concern is that real estate is not "liquid".  That is, if the real estate you have invested in does not seem to be doing well and you want to get out of it, it can take a very long time to sell your property. Other investments can be sold as quickly as making a phone call. Therefore, even if you are aware that the value of your house or even the apartment building you bought is dropping, it is not always feasible to quickly sell such property. And while you are waiting for a buyer, you will be watching the value continue to drop. Also, even considering what you might hear on a late-night infomercial on TV, it is safe to say that it takes a little bit more than $25 a month to invest in real estate.

We consider gold and collectibles as one category with real estate because they are physical items that one collects. You buy up real estate expecting to either make a quick profit by selling it again at a higher price or make a small profit each month through rental. You buy gold and other collectibles with either the thought of making a long-term profit or just for the fun of it. People can collect anything of gold to see what it will be worth in the future the same as they can a Renoir painting or even Barbie dolls. Any kind of collecting of items should be done with the understanding that you are doing it for the enjoyment of owning these things and fully understanding that it may never, at least in your life time, increase in value. With this in mind, remember that we want to invest our money to see actual real growth in a safe manner.

# Mutual Funds

A mutual fund is a collection of different stocks and other types of investments that you buy along with a group of other people. The idea is that by going in with other people, you can all afford to jump into investing in a bigger way and also meet their minimum investment requirements. Some mutual funds are discussed under Pension Plans (see below). Mutual funds were created by brokers who realized that they could make a great deal more money in fees and expenses if they only took on clients who would invest at least $1,000. If they have 40 people investing a minimum of $1,000 in a month, they make more money than if they have 40 people investing only $100 in a month. In other words, dealing with the small investor was not worth their time and effort because they were looking for a very large income from other people's money.

However, it has been interesting to watch as the initial amount has been dropped over the past two years. In fact, now there are brokerages, though very few, who will take as little as $500 for an initial investment. Will this amount go lower? We do not know but it seems to be going in the other direction. Fewer and fewer brokers are willing to do the very small transaction.

With some mutual funds, you have a limited amount of control over which companies (or types of companies) you will be investing in and, in others, you have no control. The mutual fund buying and selling will be controlled by your broker to a greater or lesser extent. Again, you must answer the question of whether you want someone else making the decisions concerning your money and whether you are willing to spend a very small amount of time to handle your finances yourself in order to have control of the situation as well as save on the fees. You can find mutual funds with excellent track records considering that excellent means up to 30% growth a year. But what will their track record be next year? If their record declines, you will need to be ready to make a change. The broker handling your investments may be excellent, but what will happen if there is a personnel change? Again, you will need to make a change. Unfortunately, we have had many attendees at our seminars who came because the Southeast Asian market collapse caused their mutual fund to drop in value way below what they had initially invested in it.

Mutual Funds can give you more diversity in your investments more quickly in that you would have shares in over a hundred different companies. In fact, the average American mutual fund is in 180 different businesses. They do this to create diversity for your investment, but there is such a thing as too much diversity which we will explain later. One thing we do know is that no matter what type of fund you ask for (safe, risky, retirement oriented, income, etc.), about a third of your money will go into very safe stock such as we will be talking about, a third into relatively safe stock that has a little risk, and a third into highly risky stock. The idea is that if the risky businesses fail, you will have the growth from the safe ones to offset those losses. But personally, we are not interested in just breaking even with our money.

And for this diversity you are: (1) paying a management fee (monthly expense fee) even when your investment loses value; (2) facing personnel changes that may make better or worse decisions for you; and (3) risking your money on a huge portfolio with some very risky stock that you have no choice over. Of course, for our purposes, the major problem (4) is that a minimum investment of at least $1,000 is usually necessary. At $25 a month it will take you over 3 years to save enough to start investing and that 3 years can be very discouraging. Recently, some mutual fund businesses have lowered their minimum investment to as little as $500 a month, but this is contingent on investing $500 every month, no matter what your situation. These high initial costs are why so many investment clubs have sprung up. Obviously, a group of people pooling their assets can meet the minimum dollar requirement and afford to jump into a mutual fund quickly.

Investing in one of the hundreds of Mutual Funds available takes a lot more research than the average person usually wants to do. To intelligently invest in a Mutual Fund, you need to fully understand front-end loaded funds (admission fee of as high as 8% plus the usual management fee), back-end loaded funds (up to 8% fee when you sell plus the usual management fee), closed-end funds (you buy at a discount when it is offered but cannot sell unless they allow it and you still pay the management fee), and many other terms which seem to be increasing monthly. All of these different funds were created to make you think that you are getting a good deal ("Gee, I don't have to pay a fee until I sell when I can afford that 8% fee because all of my investments will have gone up!"). If you do not understand them, you can end up losing a great deal more than you put in originally.

Probably your biggest concern, after the safety of your money, should be how much you can make. That is, the very best producing mutual funds these days are showing a 20% to 23% growth. Yes, you can get into some extremely risky ones that will occasionally show an even higher increase but we could never recommend that you risk your future like that. When investing in the safe companies we are talking about, you should be making an average of **50% to 100%** (sometimes even more) per year growth in the value of your stock.

We know it sounds impossible, but you should read every word of any contract you ever sign including your mutual fund agreement. Unfortunately, because they are so difficult to understand, most people do not. The result is, as we have seen quite often in our seminars, people who believe that they cannot ever lose the money the originally put into the mutual fund. You can lose it all!

## Investment Clubs

Investment clubs have become quite famous in this decade thanks to the Beardstown Ladies, a group of older women from the town of Beardstown, Illionois, some retired and some not, who formed a group to learn more about investing and to pool their money in order to meet the minimum investment (usually $1,000) required by brokers. They became famous because they were able to choose stocks and investments in which their return was much higher than the Standard & Poor 500 (S&P 500), a cumulative index of the best rated stocks on the market. Perhaps the major reason that our public thought this feat was worth a book about the Beardstown ladies is that it seemed amazing to some segments of our population that anyone, including women (and in this case, even elderly women) can learn how to build their financial portfolio and take care of their own money. We do not find this at all amazing. Anyone,

45

regardless of race, sex, religion, or age, can learn to take care of their own finances very easily. The secret is that one word in the previous sentence, "learn". If you are not willing to learn, then you cannot do it. Knowledge gives you power, therefore, you should continually be learning new things, including how to increase your financial worth. Besides, isn't it fun watching your investments grow?

What do we dislike about a club? Do you really want to trust your money to other people? These co-authors own four businesses between the two of them; and yet, he has no partial ownership in her businesses and she has no partial ownership in his businesses. Why? Because too many good friendships (and marriages) have broken up due to joint business ventures. In a club situation, everyone votes on which investments to participate in and you must go along with the majority vote. How many of you are working for a boss who is making the wrong decisions for the company and there is nothing you can do about it? Do you want to get into that same kind of situation with your investments? When you are investing your own money, it is the same as having your own business. Therefore, you can and should make your own decisions. For some people, a club makes it easier to sit back and let others make decisions for you and thus, we suppose, to have someone else to blame for any mistakes made. However, we have found that clubs are having a problem with members dropping out because they do not like doing the calculations involved every month. If you are in a club having a problem with drop-outs, consider letting your math-fearing members use our method of research so as not to scare them away just because of numbers.

Aside from the question of who is controlling your money, most clubs go through regular brokers who are charging you fees and monthly expenses. Granted, they listen to the suggestions made by their brokers and, therefore, seem to be getting their money's worth. But you can do what a broker will do for you, and better than they will do it, on your own and for free. However, as we have said, the law requires that you deal with a broker and we, only when necessary, use only discount brokers in our method. Keep in mind that you will not be paying a broker anything for the vast majority of your investments. The reasons for this will be explained shortly.

## IRA's and Employee Pension Plans

The current maximum yearly amount you can put into your IRA (Individual Retirement Account) is up to $4,000 *per couple.* As this is a maximum, you can open one for much less. If your budget allows for this, we encourage you to do so. An IRA may not have the liquidity or the high growth of the stock market in that you will pay penalties for early withdrawal under age 59 1/2, but it is a guaranteed source of income for retirement. Be aware that you are still putting your money into a mutual fund. Currently, most IRA's are averaging only about a 5% return.

You may work for a company that offers an employee pension plan such as a 401K plan. With this type of plan, you contribute a set amount from each pay check into a professionally managed fund. These plans allow you to defer or put off paying taxes in the year your money was earned while still earning interest on stock appreciation.

Sometimes the company also contributes a set amount. If you are working for such a company, we suggest that you take advantage of this program. Whenever your employer matches what you put into your pension plan, you should join it as their share is just free money in your pocket. However, always be aware of where the funds are being invested, i.e. stock market, mutual funds, etc. because then you need to read what we have said about each of those areas.

If your pension fund is being invested in the company you work for, you need to be particularly carefully and research how well the company is doing. We suggest you follow the method we outline in chapter IV. However, since you are working in that area already, you will have additional places to research. For instance, if you are working in the banking industry and have the opportunity to invest in your particular bank, you will want to contact the public relations department for a copy of their annual report, talk to a senior vice president about the outlook for the company, call any contacts you have at other banks to chat about the banking industry as a whole (are they being bought out, are they closing any branches, are they laying off personnel). This will give you more insight into your industry, but you will still want to follow our suggested research in chapter IV to get totally unbiased opinions also.

After all, you are probably emotionally involved in your employment to the point that you would put your own money into a company that is not necessarily a good investment, or not as good an investment as you could otherwise make. Research your employer carefully along with other stocks in the same industry and compare it to other types of industries to decide where your money will do the best for you. Any information you can collect is only useful if you can determine its validity by comparing it with other information sources.

## Stocks

Investing in the stock market got quite a bit of bad press back in 1929. One huge crash (which initially only wiped out those who had invested borrowed money that they did not have and ended up bankrupt) and the word was out - - the stock market is too risky! And yet, our method is based almost entirely on the stock market. Why? Because it is where you have the **greatest potential** for the highest gains and, if you follow our advice and use your own intelligence, you should have **very safe investments**. We could suggest a method that would have the potential for huge fast gains but would not be safe, and this we cannot condone for the beginning investor.

How safe is the stock market? We were all taught in school that the great crash of '29 led to a world-wide depression that lasted for 10 years and that we only came out of that depression because of World War II. However, if you look at the actual statistics for that time period (from Value Line), you will find that the Dow Jones Industrial Average companies only dropped for three years following the crash. They then quickly climbed to their previous high point, before the crash, by the end of the 7th year. Yes, there were high-risk companies that went out of business, but these strong companies in the Dow Jones quickly recovered and went on to earn good profits during this great depression. Those are the type of businesses we will be looking for to invest our money in.

We feel that the public needs to know about the great opportunities available through our stock market. You have as much right to increase your wealth as anyone else even if you are starting from a smaller base. It is only our individual greed that says "it won't do me any good to invest just $25, it would take too long". Too long for what? Have you been given one month to live? It is **greed** speaking when you feel it's not worth it because you will only have $100,000 when you retire instead of $1,000,000. It is **sensible** when you feel $100,000 is better than ending up with just social security.

And learn from the past mistakes of others: **Invest only what you can afford to lose**, not everything you own including your first born! This is true of anything you invest in. After all, even banks have been known to close leaving their savings accounts to pay out only a fraction of what their owners had put in. And too many small businesses have gone under because of trying to keep the company open after it had already stopped breathing! Finally, invest only what you can afford to lose, because we personally know that there are lots of things to enjoy in life right now. You do not want to scrimp and save every penny just for retirement. You have to enjoy life now also.

We will be investing in **common stock** instead of preferred stock for several reasons. A business will only issue a limited number of shares of preferred stock, there is no reinvestment plan for it, usually no dividends are paid, and it will have limited growth as compared with common stock.

The purpose of this book is to increase your capital. However, having lived and worked all over this world, we both feel very patriotic (we realize how old fashioned this sounds) about the United States. We firmly believe in the capitalistic system that gives us the right to start our own small businesses (90% of businesses in this country are five or fewer employees). As we both come from early pioneer stock, we also firmly believe in our lives only having a purpose if we are taking care of ourselves and then, with our success, helping the less fortunate. Thus, we would like to point out that when you invest your money to build your own capital, you are also helping the backbone of this country, private enterprise. When we are young and struggling, there seems to be nothing left to even help ourselves. Then, when we have learned a great deal more, we may not have a lot of money, but we have time to volunteer to help others. But eventually, through 90% hard work and 10% luck and intelligence, we have enough to share with others financially. So, help yourself and your children and your country and your neighbors by investing in the stock market and in American companies.

## III.  HOW TO SAVE MONEY

## After Paying The Bills, How Can I Invest In Anything?

One of the main reasons people use for not investing is that they have nothing left after paying all the bills.  There are obvious solutions to this such as taking on a part-time second job (the co-author once worked three jobs at one time, however, she was single at the time).  But usually you do not need more money than you currently have to start investing.

An often overlooked fact is that stocks can sell for only a few dollars or over a hundred dollars per share.  We are not talking about penny stocks that are here today and gone tomorrow.  But the price of a share of stock, in even a huge company like Coca-Cola, can vary from $40 to $150 a share, give or take a few dollars.  In the next chapter, we will talk about how to choose which stocks to invest in.  For now, all you need to know is that you will need about $75 to get started.  "Wait a minute!!!  You said I only needed $25 or less a month to invest!!"  Okay, so you need a little bit more to get started with and then you follow up with the $25 every month.

**Our method is this:  You only need to invest in <u>one</u> share of stock (let's say about $40 worth) to get started and then invest $25 a month (or less) which, along with reinvestment of dividends and splits, will give your money tremendous growth.**

Even using our method, it is still the law that a broker has to do the transaction for you. But we will be telling you how to use a discount broker (see below) to buy just one share of stock at $40 plus about $35 in for a one-time only broker fee.  After your initial investment, you no longer need to pay a broker, unless buying stock in an additional company.  We will also be explaining how to make your initial investment directly through the company you are buying in order to avoid broker fees and expenses entirely. To start with, let's concentrate on how much you can comfortably afford to save each month.

**1.  How Much Per Month**.  On the cover of this book, it is clearly stated "on $25 a month (or less)".  The methods we are going to be talking about can be used for any dollar amount whether you can afford $10 a month or $10,000 a month.  Only you can decide how much that monthly dollar amount should be.  The examples we will be using in this book are all based on $25 as that is an amount that just about anyone has available each month. However, if you are a student mowing lawns or a single parent working two jobs, you can still use these methods but at a lower monthly amount, even only $5 a month. You see, the rate or percent at which your money grows will be the same no matter how much you are contributing; it just may take a little longer to get where you want to go. But you will get there! If you invest in a strong, safe company that is showing its investors a 60% annual growth rate, you will get that 60% whether you are investing $25 a month or $2,000 a month. In other words, it may take you longer, but you are being treated exactly the same as everyone else.

It does not matter whether you are investing $5 a month or $2,000 a month. What is important is that you invest the same amount EVERY SINGLE MONTH! I can remember years ago setting up a Christmas Savings Account so I would have enough to buy presents for the holiday. But guess what? It seemed that each week (or month) I just did not have that $5 to put into the bank. Thus, the first (and only) rule of saving, which you have probably heard many times, is **pay yourself first**. No one else is going to take care of your finances, nor should they. Only you can save your own money.

You need to go over your budget and see how much you can afford to invest each month (not weekly) without going hungry. Go through your check book for the past few months and make a list of every bill you paid and every item you bought for each month.  From this you can get an idea of what your regular monthly bills average as well as how much you tend to spend on extras.  Then make up a typical monthly budget for your family showing the dollar amount you spend for rent/mortgage, groceries, gas, electricity, etc.  Then write down what your paycheck is each month plus any other money that you get every month.

Hopefully, this list will show that you earn more than you spend.  If not, this would be a good time to look more closely at your charge card habits.  Or maybe you just need to cut back a little on your expenses.  Cut out the lunches and take a bag lunch, stop renting videos for awhile, make an effort to cut back on electricity usage, etc.  In the end, you want to have a few dollars left over not for you (all of these bills every month are for you) but rather for your future.  After all, if you just cut out one family meal at McDonald's each month, you would have saved enough money to get started. The end result from your list should be a dollar amount that you can afford to invest each month comfortably, even if it is only $5.

For ease in understanding, we will refer to $25 a month throughout this book even though you may have a different amount in mind.  In order to use this method correctly and to **build** your financial portfolio, you must treat this $25 as a regular monthly bill, the same as you would your electric bill. You must have a specific day each month that you will invest this $25. Perhaps when you write out and mail the check for your electric bill, you could write out your savings check. Or when you send in your monthly mortgage payment, write out your monthly savings check. Also, keep in mind that some companies you are interested in investing in will offer the option of direct withdrawal from your own savings account. For instance, you can buy stock directly from General Electric and have a certain dollar amount taken from your savings account each month.

We told you this method does not take a lot of your time. Therefore, after you have started your investment plan, pick one day a year (we suggest on New Years Day), to go over your budget and see if you can increase this amount. If your family budget will not tolerate an increase, that's okay. And if an emergency comes up, its okay to cut your monthly amount back. HOWEVER, if you must cut back, do not tell yourself it will only be this once. Cut back to $10, or whatever you can **easily** save out each month, until you are sure you can safely increase to $25 again. And do not increase your monthly amount unless you are sure that, for the foreseeable future at least, you will be able to maintain that monthly amount. We want you to enjoy your investments so choose a monthly amount that will work well for you, not an amount that will be too difficult for you. Just like in smoking a cigarette or having a drink at a certain time every day, being **consistent** is very important in creating your savings habit. If you get used to paying yourself each month, it will soon be a habit that you will not even think about. So pay yourself first.

**2. Start a savings account**. Yes, we told you a savings account is much too slow. But if you decide to invest in a company that will not do the first purchase for you, you will have to go to a broker with enough money to cover the cost of one share plus his transaction fee. Let's say this first share will cost you $75. For some of you, sitting down and writing a check for $75 may be relatively easy. But if your budget will not stand that sudden jolt, put your monthly $25 into a bank savings account. After all, we are only talking about saving for three months to get the $75 you need to start with. Three months will give you plenty of time to do the research required in the next chapter. Even if you can only save $5 a month, it will take you only fifteen months to get started on your investment plan. And fifteen months is not long when you check our examples and see what the long term results will be. In fact, waiting and building that first initial investment can be as much fun as planning and waiting for your vacation - - half the fun in going on a great vacation is in the planning. Also, if you do have to take several months to get started investing, try writing down what you get for interest each month from your monthly bank statement. Then when you do start investing and getting quarterly reports, you can compare the figures with what your money was doing in your savings account and have a very big smile on your face (smiling is a very healthy thing to do). Even most teenagers, if they are willing, can save $5 a month.

We will talk later about how to actually do the investing. The important thing to remember is that you will buy your initial share or shares directly from the company, when possible. If that particular company will not do the first purchase for you, you will have to go to a discount broker to buy one share in order to get started. Thereafter, no matter how you bought the first share, you will be buying all future shares directly from the company and saving those broker fees and expenses.

# IV.  THE METHOD


## Now That I've Got A Little Stash, What Do I Do With It?

As soon as you put your first $25 into your new savings account, it is time to start THE METHOD.  Basically, The Method is picking out **what** stock to invest in.  Note that we said stock, not stocks.  We all know the expression "don't put all your eggs in one basket", however, we also feel that one egg is better than no eggs! When should you **diversify**?  Invest only in one company until you have 50 shares of it and then let it continue to build on itself while you start investing your $25 a month in another company. We recommend never investing in more then six companies.     The   Wall   Street   Journal recommends no more then ten companies when using this type of safe investing and the Value Line recommends from six to eight.  Because we are going to be investing in only the safest of businesses,   we   do   not   need   so   much diversification.

Why should you consider diversifying at all? Any economy is cyclical meaning that sometimes the economy is good and sometimes it is not so good. It also means that the economy as a whole can be doing fine, but a particular industry is not doing so well. You could decide to invest in an oil company realizing how important oil is for every day transportation as well as all of the synthetics we live off of. But it only takes one oil spill to drop the value of your investment overnight. In all probability, your stock will go right back up again and continue to grow, but while it is down in value it is nice to have other investments that are still doing very well. That is, we are talking about long-term investing. But if an emergency came up and you needed to sell some stock, you want to make sure that at least one of your companies is doing well even if our economy as a whole is not.

The economy in a particular section of the country will also have its ups and downs. This can affect the value of some stock and it can affect your wallet. Finally, your own personal economics can be stronger at times and weaker at times depending on whether you are getting more overtime pay, develop a second source of income, lose your job, etc. Since all of these things can effect your investment plan and the price of your stock, it is a good idea to diversify. Then, if you suddenly need some money for a family emergency and must sell some stock to raise the money, chances are that at least one of your investments can be sold at a profit or sold for more than what you originally paid for it.

Please be wary of over-diversification which mutual funds do by buying into so many companies. The average American mutual fund is invested in an average of 140 entities. When investing in *safe* companies, we suggest owning stock in no more than 6 companies.

Which company should you start with? We want it to be safe to protect our savings but we want it to be growing so that we do not have to do all the work. If it doesn't grow, you might as well keep your money in the savings account or under your mattress!

To determine which stock is right for you, we need to do a little research. Don't panic! We said **a little**. You do not need to become an expert in the stock market to invest in it. And you do not need to spend a lot of time. You can spend two hours at the library and pick out your first stock or you can spend a week. But, again, this book is meant for people who do not find investing all that interesting (only the resulting increase in your money) and want to spend as little time as possible on this activity. There are two excellent resources, both available for free at your public library, that you will need to look at: Value Line's Investment Survey and The Wall Street Journal. Sounds pretty scary, doesn't it? Especially when you get to the library and find that the Value Line's Investment Survey is a huge book and each daily Wall Street Journal is the thickest newspaper you've ever seen! It's okay - - you are not going to read these, only use certain information in them. But before using either of them, you need to start with the first step.

**1. Gut Instinct.** "Gut instinct??!! How can I use gut instinct on something I know nothing about??!!" Don't underestimate yourself! You know the market place much better than you think you do. You probably know which stores to shop at to get the best bargains. And you probably know which brand to buy to get the results you want. Even teenagers know which video systems sell the best or which brand of clothes out sells all the others year in and year out. In fact, if you as an adult are considering these types of companies, you should get a teens opinion first. This is what we mean by gut instinct - - choosing things that you personally know about and have experience with.

Sit down with paper and pencil and start listing the things you really like using. What brand products do you always use because you feel they are the best on the market? What stores do you shop at because you feel they are the best? What is (or would be if you could afford it) your favorite vacation destination? What is your favorite car? Your favorite restaurant? Also, only look at the large companies as, historically, the stock of larger companies has always outperformed the small company stocks. If you feel good about a certain product or service, chances are that part of the reason is that it is large and well-known making other people also feel good about it.

On your piece of paper, you want to make two columns. One should be headed "essentials" and the other "non-essentials". That is, there are certain things that we have to have in order to survive. These are essential industries. Everything else is non-essential.

The reason we make a distinction between essential and non-essential things is that the first group will always be necessary in our civilization. We must have food and drink and, in this age, our gas as well as fuel (for heating and to run the car) to just get by in today's civilization. That means that no matter what happens, short of a nuclear war, people will always buy these things. Even if there were to be a severe depression/recession, people still need food and drink, they need to keep warm and cook their food, and they need to get to any possible work to earn money. Certainly this is a worst case scenario, but it makes these companies the safest to invest in. Other industries, leisure, manufacturing and service industries, etc. would be the first to collapse during a major national or international problem. Even during a small recession with some people losing their jobs, the first things to be cut out of the family budget are vacations, that extra wide-screen TV, eating at restaurants, buying a new car or house, etc. Since economics will always be cyclical in our world, we concentrate on buying stock in the essential areas until we have our nest egg and then we can diversify into the non-essential companies.

So start with two columns on a piece of paper, one being essential and one being non-essential. Then list each of your products and services that you particularly like under one of those headings. It is a small organizing step that will be very useful when you are ready to diversify because diversifying means going into a completely different area. If you start by investing in a company in the food industry, you would want to diversify into another area such as utilities or shelter.

However, deciding whether a business is essential or not can be tricky. For instance, there are two types of pharmaceutical companies: regular and high-tech (although we usually think of high-tech as being computers and software). The regular ones make our aspirin, bandages, etc. while the high-tech ones are into research and development which is always a high risk area in any industry.

Having a cyclical economy is why we use older, well established, large companies like Coca-Cola and General Electric as examples of what $25 a month can do for you. We are not recommending Coca-Cola or General Electric but only giving you real examples of what your small investment can turn into. If you are trying to teach your children about investing and they seem a little uninterested, try showing them the examples we have created to demonstrate to them how their small amount can grow without them having to do anything for it. Remember that you should never invest in any company, no matter what your "gut instinct" is or what your friends say or even your broker tells you, until you go to the library and do a little research.

**2. Research.** After you have listed all your preferred products and services, choose several of the ones you are personally familiar with and that are the most well-known to begin your research with. If you have the time and the inclination, you can certainly research every one of the companies on your list. But, again, we are assuming you do not want to spend lots of your spare time doing this.

When you get to the library, you are going to first use the Value Line's Investment Survey (this can be purchased or used online but is very expensive). Remember also that you can make copies at the library of the pages you want to study further. The reasons for the Value Line's importance are that everything you need to know about a certain company is on one page, including an 18 year history of highs and lows, and it is relatively easy to understand. If you do not easily understand some parts of it, do not worry as those parts are not as important anyway unless you are trying to make riskier investments in order to make a fast buck. Here is what you need to look for:

a. As in 1 above, look for companies you are familiar with and feel confident in. Then make sure they are large and well-known before continuing your research. You want to invest only in companies that have at least a strong 10 year history. It is always better to invest $100 in a good stock than to buy 50 shares of a $2 stock that has extremely little chance of helping your portfolio.

b. Remember, you want a stock with good value. Value stocks have always out-performed stocks that are growing too quickly (growth stocks). Osborne Computer developed the first lap top computer and was a fast growing stock, but it could not keep up with its competition and in three years was out of business even though it had tremendous potential and was, at the time, recommended more than Microsoft was (they went public the same year). A growth stock has the *potential* to make you a lot of money but, unfortunately, the history of growth stocks proves that value stocks are much, much safer and *will* make you a lot of money. **A good value stock should show increasing earnings over the previous five years at least, preferably ten years.** We will explain later how to tell the difference between value and growth stocks and stocks that are both value and growth stocks.

    c.  Look for a company that is constantly expanding its market by creating new products or moving into other countries. A business cannot keep increasing profits if it is not growing. But it is important to keep in mind that growth can also be a bad thing. You will need to check out whether a company is trying to grow too quickly and is, therefore, headed for trouble, or if the company is having strong, normal growth. We will be talking about how and where to find this information.

    d.  If the top management of a company owns large percentages of stock in it, you can assume they would not invest their money in a problem company. Likewise, if you read or hear something about top management selling large blocks of stock, it is time to be very careful.

    On the next page is a typical Value Line page. We are going to use General Electric as an example of how useful Value Line is and what you need to look at and understand on each page of Value Line in order to make your decision as to which stock to start your portfolio with.

    When you go to the library and ask the reference librarian for the Value Line, you will be handed a book about 4 inches thick. An edition is published once a week and added to the back of the book. Therefore, when looking for a specific company, just start at the back of the book and go through each section. Companies are listed alphabetically.

# GENERAL ELECTRIC NYSE-GE

| | | |
|---|---|---|
| RECENT PRICE **120** | P/E RATIO **36.1** (Trailing: 38.7 Median: 15.0) | RELATIVE P/E RATIO **2.41** |
| DIV'D YLD **1.3%** | VALUE LINE **1010** | |

| | |
|---|---|
| TIMELINESS **2** Raised 10/15/99 | |
| SAFETY **1** New 7/27/90 | |
| TECHNICAL **3** Lowered 4/2/99 | |
| BETA 1.25 (1.00 = Market) | |

**2002-04 PROJECTIONS**
| | Price | Gain | Ann'l Total Return |
|---|---|---|---|
| High | 150 | (+25%) | 7% |
| Low | 125 | (+5%) | 3% |

**Insider Decisions**
| | N | D | J | F | M | A | M | J | J |
|---|---|---|---|---|---|---|---|---|---|
| to Buy | 0 | 0 | 0 | 0 | 0 | 0 | 0 | 0 | 0 |
| Options | 0 | 0 | 1 | 1 | 0 | 4 | 0 | 0 | 2 |
| to Sell | 1 | 0 | 1 | 1 | 0 | 3 | 0 | 0 | 7 |

**Institutional Decisions**
| | 4Q1998 | 1Q1999 | 2Q1999 |
|---|---|---|---|
| to Buy | 578 | 578 | 544 |
| to Sell | 558 | 586 | 594 |
| Hld's(000) | 1670751 | 1665454 | 1669749 |

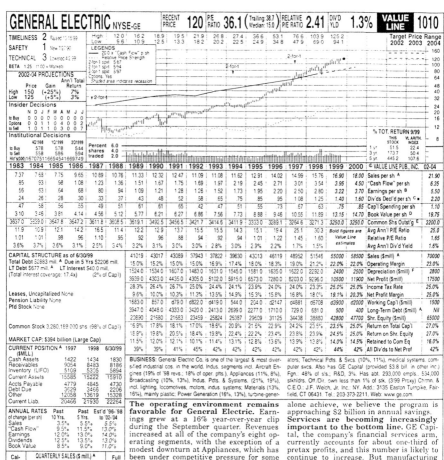

LEGENDS
20.0 x "Cash Flow" p sh
.... Relative Price Strength
2-for-1 split 5/87
2-for-1 split 5/94
2-for-1 split 5/97
Options: Yes
Shaded area indicates recession

% TOT. RETURN 9/99
| | THIS STOCK | VL ARITH. INDEX |
|---|---|---|
| 1 yr. | 51.5 | 22.4 |
| 3 yr. | 173.7 | 50.4 |
| 5 yr. | 445.2 | 107.6 |

| | 1983 | 1984 | 1985 | 1986 | 1987 | 1988 | 1989 | 1990 | 1991 | 1992 | 1993 | 1994 | 1995 | 1996 | 1997 | 1998 | 1999 | 2000 | © VALUE LINE PUB., INC. 02-04 |
|---|---|---|---|---|---|---|---|---|---|---|---|---|---|---|---|---|---|---|---|
| Sales per sh ^A | 7.37 | 7.68 | 7.75 | 9.65 | 10.89 | 10.76 | 11.33 | 12.32 | 12.47 | 11.09 | 11.08 | 11.62 | 12.91 | 14.02 | 14.99 | 15.76 | 16.90 | 18.00 | 21.90 |
| "Cash Flow" per sh | .85 | .93 | .98 | 1.08 | 1.23 | 1.36 | 1.51 | 1.67 | 1.75 | 1.69 | 1.97 | 2.19 | 2.45 | 2.71 | 3.01 | 3.54 | 3.95 | 4.50 | 6.35 |
| Earnings per sh ^B | .56 | .63 | .64 | .68 | .80 | .94 | 1.09 | 1.21 | 1.28 | 1.26 | 1.52 | 1.73 | 1.95 | 2.20 | 2.50 | 2.80 | 3.22 | 3.70 | 5.50 |
| Div'ds Decl'd per sh ^C■ | .24 | .26 | .28 | .30 | .33 | .37 | .43 | .48 | .52 | .58 | .65 | .75 | .85 | .95 | 1.08 | 1.25 | 1.40 | 1.60 | 2.20 |
| Cap'l Spending per sh | .47 | .58 | .56 | .55 | .49 | .51 | .61 | .61 | .65 | .42 | .47 | .51 | .55 | .73 | .67 | .63 | .75 | .85 | 1.10 |
| Book Value per sh ^D | 3.10 | 3.46 | 3.81 | 4.14 | 4.56 | 5.12 | 5.77 | 6.21 | 6.27 | 6.86 | 7.56 | 7.73 | 8.88 | 9.46 | 10.55 | 11.89 | 13.15 | 14.70 | 19.75 |
| Common Shs Outst'g ^E | 3637.0 | 3659.0 | 3647.8 | 3647.2 | 3611.8 | 3608.5 | 3619.1 | 3492.5 | 3456.5 | 3421.7 | 3414.6 | 3411.9 | 3333.0 | 3289.1 | 3264.6 | 3271.3 | 3250.0 | 3250.0 | 3200.0 |
| Avg Ann'l P/E Ratio | 11.9 | 10.9 | 12.1 | 14.2 | 16.5 | 11.4 | 12.2 | 12.9 | 13.7 | 15.5 | 15.5 | 14.3 | 15.1 | 19.4 | 25.1 | 30.3 | Bold figures are Value Line estimates | | 25.0 |
| Relative P/E Ratio | 1.01 | 1.01 | .98 | .96 | 1.10 | .95 | .92 | .96 | .88 | .94 | .92 | .94 | 1.01 | 1.22 | 1.45 | 1.60 | | | 1.65 |
| Avg Ann'l Div'd Yield | 3.6% | 3.7% | 3.6% | 3.1% | 2.5% | 3.4% | 3.2% | 3.1% | 3.0% | 3.0% | 2.8% | 3.0% | 2.9% | 2.2% | 1.7% | 1.5% | | | 1.6% |

**CAPITAL STRUCTURE as of 6/30/99**
Total Debt $2883 mill. ^A Due in 5 Yrs $2206 mill.
LT Debt $677 mill. ^A LT Interest $40.0 mill.
(Total interest coverage: 17.4x) (2% of Cap'l)

Leases, Uncapitalized None
Pension Liability None
Pfd Stock None

Common Stock 3,260,189,000 shs (98% of Cap'l)

MARKET CAP: $394 billion (Large Cap)

| | 1989 | 1990 | 1991 | 1992 | 1993 | 1994 | 1995 | 1996 | 1997 | 1998 | 1999 | 2000 | |
|---|---|---|---|---|---|---|---|---|---|---|---|---|---|
| Sales ($mill) ^A | 41019 | 43017 | 43089 | 37943 | 37822 | 39630 | 43013 | 46119 | 48952 | 51545 | 55000 | 58500 | 70000 |
| Operating Margin | 15.0% | 15.2% | 15.0% | 15.0% | 16.9% | 17.4% | 18.0% | 18.3% | 19.0% | 21.2% | 22.0% | 22.0% | 23.0% |
| Depreciation ($mill) ^F | 1524.0 | 1534.0 | 1607.0 | 1483.0 | 1631.0 | 1545.0 | 1581.0 | 1635.0 | 1622.0 | 2292.0 | 2400 | 2500 | 2800 |
| Net Profit ($mill) | 3939.0 | 4303.0 | 4435.0 | 4305.0 | 5102.0 | 5915.0 | 6573.0 | 7280.0 | 8203.0 | 9296.0 | 10500 | 11900 | 17500 |
| Income Tax Rate | 28.3% | 26.4% | 26.7% | 25.0% | 24.4% | 24.1% | 23.9% | 24.0% | 24.0% | 23.3% | 25.0% | 25.0% | 25.0% |
| Net Profit Margin | 9.6% | 10.0% | 10.3% | 11.3% | 13.5% | 14.9% | 15.3% | 15.8% | 16.8% | 18.0% | 19.1% | 20.3% | 25.0% |
| Working Cap'l ($mill) | 1683.0 | 857.0 | d79.0 | d822.0 | d419.0 | 544.0 | 204.0 | d2147 | d4881 | d6708 | d3900 | d2000 | 1500 |
| Long-Term Debt ($mill) ^A | 3947.0 | 4048.0 | 4333.0 | 3420.0 | 2413.0 | 2699.0 | 2277.0 | 1710.0 | 729.0 | 681.0 | 500 | 400 | Nil |
| Shr. Equity ($mill) | 20890 | 21580 | 21683 | 23459 | 25824 | 26387 | 29509 | 31125 | 34438 | 38880 | 42800 | 47700 | 65000 |
| Return on Total Cap'l | 16.9% | 17.8% | 18.1% | 17.0% | 18.6% | 20.9% | 21.5% | 22.9% | 24.2% | 23.5% | 23.5% | 25.0% | 27.0% |
| Return on Shr. Equity | 18.9% | 19.8% | 20.5% | 18.4% | 19.8% | 22.4% | 22.2% | 23.4% | 23.8% | 23.9% | 24.5% | 25.0% | 27.0% |
| Retained to Com Eq | 11.5% | 12.0% | 12.1% | 10.1% | 11.4% | 13.1% | 12.8% | 13.6% | 13.9% | 13.8% | 14.0% | 14.5% | 16.0% |
| All Div'ds to Net Prof | 39% | 39% | 41% | 45% | 42% | 42% | 42% | 42% | 42% | 42% | 44% | 42% | 42% |

**CURRENT POSITION ^A** ($MILL.)
| | 1997 | 1998 | 6/30/99 |
|---|---|---|---|
| Cash Assets | 1422 | 1434 | 1830 |
| Receivables | 9054 | 8483 | 8186 |
| Inventory (LIFO) | 5109 | 5305 | 5894 |
| **Current Assets** | 15585 | 15222 | 15910 |
| Accts Payable | 4779 | 4845 | 4730 |
| Debt Due | 3629 | 3466 | 2206 |
| Other | 12058 | 13619 | 15328 |
| **Current Liab.** | 20466 | 21930 | 22264 |

**ANNUAL RATES**
| of change (per sh) | Past 10 Yrs. | Past 5 Yrs. | Est'd '96-'98 to '02-'04 |
|---|---|---|---|
| Sales | 3.5% | 5.5% | 5.5% |
| "Cash Flow" | 9.5% | 11.5% | 13.0% |
| Earnings | 12.0% | 13.0% | 14.0% |
| Dividends | 12.5% | 13.5% | 13.0% |
| Book Value | 8.5% | 9.0% | 11.0% |

| Cal-endar | QUARTERLY SALES ($mill.) ^A | | | | Full Year |
|---|---|---|---|---|---|
| | Mar.31 | Jun.30 | Sep.30 | Dec.31 | |
| 1996 | 9742 | 11520 | 11478 | 13379 | 46119 |
| 1997 | 10522 | 12620 | 11698 | 14112 | 48952 |
| 1998 | 11408 | 13217 | 12075 | 14846 | 51546 |
| 1999 | 11796 | 13966 | 13228 | 16010 | 55000 |
| 2000 | 12600 | 15000 | 14300 | 16600 | 58500 |

| Cal-endar | EARNINGS PER SHARE ^B | | | | Full Year |
|---|---|---|---|---|---|
| | Mar.31 | Jun.30 | Sep.30 | Dec.31 | |
| 1996 | .48 | .58 | .54 | .62 | 2.20 |
| 1997 | .51 | .66 | .62 | .71 | 2.50 |
| 1998 | .57 | .74 | .69 | .80 | 2.80 |
| 1999 | .65 | .85 | .80 | .92 | 3.22 |
| 2000 | .75 | .95 | .93 | 1.07 | 3.70 |

| Cal-endar | QUARTERLY DIVIDENDS PAID ^C■ | | | | Full Year |
|---|---|---|---|---|---|
| | Mar.31 | Jun.30 | Sep.30 | Dec.31 | |
| 1995 | .205 | .205 | .205 | .205 | .82 |
| 1996 | .23 | .23 | .23 | .23 | .92 |
| 1997 | .26 | .26 | .26 | .26 | 1.04 |
| 1998 | .30 | .30 | .30 | .30 | 1.20 |
| 1999 | .35 | .35 | .35 | | |

**BUSINESS:** General Electric Co. is one of the largest & most diversified industrial cos. in the world. Indus. segments incl. Aircraft Engines (19% of '98 revs.; 18% of oper. pfts.), Appliances (11%, 8%), Broadcasting (10%, 13%), Indus. Pdts. & Systems. (21%, 19%), incl. lighting, locomotives, motors, indus. systems; Materials (13%, 16%), mainly plastic; Power Generation (16%, 13%), turbine-generators; Technical Pdts. & Svcs. (10%, 11%), medical systems, computer svcs. Also has GE Capital (provided $3.8 bill. in other inc.) Fgn.: 48% of s/s.; R&D, 3%. Has abt. 293,000 empls., 534,000 stkhldrs. Off./Dir. own less than 1% of stk. (1999 Proxy) Chrmn. & C.E.O.: J.F. Welch, Jr. Inc.: NY. Add.: 3135 Easton Turnpike, Fairfield, CT 06431. Tel.: 203-373-2211. Web: www.ge.com.

The operating environment remains favorable for General Electric. Earnings grew at a 16% year-over-year clip during the September quarter. Revenues increased at all of the company's eight operating segments, with the exception of a modest downturn at Appliances, which has been under competitive pressure for some time now. GE's appliances have long had a reputation for quality, and innovative new products that are in the works give us confidence the problems are of the short-term variety. Operating earnings at Power Systems, on the other hand, increased 51% on 28% sales growth in the quarter, and a hefty backlog indicates this trend is likely to persist.

Quality-control initiatives are powering much of the earnings growth at GE. Indeed, the company maintains executive management positions with the sole responsibility of improving quality across all operations. The ongoing process involves rigorous statistical analysis, with the goal of eventually minimizing the number of errors in any manufacturing or service activity to 1 in 3.4 million. Although this is difficult to measure, let alone achieve, we believe the program is approaching $2 billion in annual savings.

Services are becoming increasingly important to the bottom line. GE Capital, the company's financial services arm, currently accounts for about one-third of pretax profits, and this number is likely to continue to increase. But manufacturing service revenues are also growing rapidly. With the company's excellent reputation for quality, it is not difficult to sell service contracts along with an order for high-tech medical equipment, for instance. Moreover, these contracts provide a high-margin, recurring-revenue stream, which should help minimize the effect of economic downturns on the bottom line.

GE shares are timely. However, investors with an eye to 2002-2004 will probably want to wait for a pullback in the stock price before making new commitments. Earnings growth will likely remain in the mid-teens for the foreseeable future, but the relatively high P/E multiple currently accorded the stock leaves scant margin for error in the event of a rise in interest rates or a general market correction.
*Noah Goldner* *October 22, 1999*

(A) Revs. and balance-sheet data excl. fin. serv. sub.; revs. also excl. other inc. (B) Based on avg. shs. Excl. nonrecur. losses: '91, 82c; '93, 26c; Excl. gains (loss) from disc. oper.: '92, 13c; '93, 22c; '94, (35c). Next egs. rpt. due late Jan. (C) Next div'd mtg. abt. Dec. 20th. Goes ex abt. Dec. 26th. Approx. div'd pymt. dates: 25th of Jan., April, July, Oct. ■ Div'd reinvest. plan. (D) Incl. intang.: in '98: $9,996 mill. $3.06/sh. (E) In mill., adj. for stk. splits. (F) Mostly on an accelerated basis.

| Company's Financial Strength | A++ |
|---|---|
| Stock's Price Stability | 90 |
| Price Growth Persistence | 100 |
| Earnings Predictability | 100 |

To subscribe call 1-800-833-0046.

Do not be frightened by all that small print jammed into such a tiny space as we are only going to be using a few parts of this prodigious material. The rest of these facts are for brokers and consultants and people who want to spend a great deal more time on their investments and who are willing to take a lot more risk with their capital.

Probably the easiest place to start is the written description in the lower right corner. This is written by their staff expert in that particular industry. It is not actual fact as no one can predict the future, but it is the opinion of an expert who spends his whole life studying these areas (isn't it nice to get an expert's opinion for free). This description always includes what the company has been doing recently, what it is expected to do, and how certain activities (such as new products, cost cutting, etc.) should affect the future of the stock. This is one area to read carefully.

In the upper left corner is an item called SAFETY and, for General Electric, it is listed as "1" (very high). A 1 or 2 is acceptable for us.

The chart in the upper right corner of the Value Line page shows the history of the stock including splits and the increase in value. This is a good visualization of how the company has been doing. The other information can be very interesting but not necessarily important in making your decision. As with the companies annual report, you need to be somewhat skeptical of dollar amounts reported as the company will do what it can to make the figures "look good". Basically, **we want to know that this company has been increasing in value over the last 10 years (stable and safe) and has had good dividends and splits (your money grows without your effort)**. Of course, you may find yourself becoming more and more interested in these reports and wanting to read and understand more of this information which *Adding To Your Financial Portfolio* does.

You want to invest in a company whose chart is showing an upward trend over at least the last 10 years. You also want to see a history of consecutive splits. That is, for General Electric you see a 2-for-1 split in 1994 and 1997. As of this writing, GE has also announced another split for 2000. In other words, about every 3 years their stock splits. These are additional shares for your portfolio that you do not have to pay for. Your money is growing all by itself.

A board of directors decides to have a split in order to lower the cost per share so that more investors will buy the shares (like getting a 2-for-1 special at the grocery store). They have to announce the split several weeks before it happens and you will hear about it in the news if it is a large company. Let's say that you bought one share of GE for $100. On the day of the split, you now have two shares, but each is now only worth $50. Did you make any money? Not now, but you will. That is why we want to see that consecutive history. We can guess that in another three years, GE's stock price will have climbed back to $100 a share so that you now have two shares each worth $100.

Most importantly, you want to check along the bottom of this page (the footnotes) to see if it says "Div'd Reinvest. Plan Available". It may not say that it does. Either way, you want to call the home office phone number listed half way down the page at the end of the "Business" section. Ask for "investor relations". Ask them if they have a dividend reinvestment plan available. If they do not, you do not want to invest in this company.

Dividends are declared by the Board of Directors to give something back to their investors. You want to sign up for this plan. Then instead of receiving a quarterly check for the dividend, it will be put back in to buy you more stock. Because we are looking for very safe investments that have very large growth, the dividends will usually be very small (as in 15 cents or less). Even with GE paying dividends of 35 cents per share, it would take a long time to buy another share. So if dividends are so unimportant, why do we consider it a major criteria for investing? Because usually, if a company has dividend reinvestments, they also have a "direct cash purchase" plan. You will need to ask the Investor Services about this.

Direct cash purchase means that you can buy additional stock directly from the company and avoid dealing with a stock broker again. This is very important and where you get the huge growth. By being able to add $25 each month to your account (without fees and expenses) you are making your portfolio grow quickly.

While you are talking to investor services, you also want to ask if you can make your first purchase of stock from them. That is, some companies such as GE will allow you to buy your first stock directly from them if you will start with a minimum of $250. This is obviously larger than $25 a month (to start with) but will save you having to pay that initial broker fee. Some of these large, strong companies insist that you buy the **first share** from an outside source (a broker). If that is the case, you will deal with a discount broker and then make additional purchases through the company (see below).

Remember: 1. Check Value Line. 2. Call Investor Services and check for Dividend Reinvestment Plan and Direct Cash Purchase Plan. 3. Can you buy first purchase directly from company?

You should now know which company you would like to invest in. Your next research step is to look at The Wall Street Journal. The Value Line is necessary to get the history and the opinion of what the future is for this particular company. The Wall Street Journal will let us know if something has happended recently or is about to happen that we should know about.

Yes, we are talking about THE Wall Street Journal that most of us think was created for only a specialized segment of our population that watches the stock market 24 hours a day! Relax, it is just another newspaper that happens to specialize in accurate and truthful business news. It is also very educational. Again, you might find yourself reading more and more of the financial news and enjoying it more, but do not be discouraged if at first you feel like you are reading a foreign language. If you find yourself exploring The Wall Street Journal in greater depth, you will discover that the articles usually explain things carefully and simply enough for most of us to understand, *if* you ***want*** to understand more about the business of the United States as well as the rest of the world. Be advised that some people who are very serious investors also invest in foreign markets. As we said earlier, sometimes our economy is down when another countries economy is heading upward. But, as recent history has shown us, foreign investing is very risky. We also have personal feelings about investing in foreign companies when we can be helping our own American companies.

Don't worry about how BIG The Wall Street Journal is. There are only two pages you will be looking at: (1) the front page and (2) the inside cover of Section B for the Index of Businesses. Scan the front cover for any mention of the company you have decided to invest in. Then check the Index. This is an alphabetical listing of all companies mentioned in this particular issue with the page number of said article. This keeps your reading at a minimum. However, keep in mind that for some people the stock market is addictive and you could find yourself wanting to learn more. In that case, there is no better tool than The Wall Street Journal.

When you first start reading The Wall Street Journal, it may be as difficult as trying to understand a foreign language. But you can learn a great deal through osmosis. If you decide to subscribe to it and start reading it daily, you will slowly learn what is being said and what it means. It gives you today's unbiased investment, business and economic information as well as all the facts you need to do your own research in a more in-depth fashion. And if you feel more adventurous, it will benefit every citizen of this country to understand at least a little of how the business cycle operates in this country and why it operates. As much as the business cycle can be annoying when it effects our jobs and lives, it is what keeps this country the strongest in the world. If you are upset when the economy effects your job status, we suggest a socialist country where jobs are guaranteed.

The Wall Street Journal is the unbiased source you need. First, glance over the front page to look for any mention of the two or three companies you have tentatively picked out (the articles will name the company in bold print). Then look at the Index of Businesses usually located on page two of the B section. This index has all of the companies that have articles written about them in this issue listed alphabetically by company name so you can just scan for anything in the rest of the paper about your company and read those specific articles. Do not worry if during the past few weeks you see no mention of the companies you are considering. As they say, no news is good news. You have already researched the history of the company up to the current time so no mention of it only means everything is continuing as usual. However, if you find articles talking about trouble, you need to pay attention. And if you find mention of an upcoming split, you REALLY need to pay attention.

While getting started, you will need to look at the last two weeks of this daily paper to see what has been going on. You might learn that your third choice is going to split next week making it necessary to decide whether to move that company up to your first choice or not. If your choice is now selling at $150 and is due to split on the first of next month, you would be wise to wait until the official split so that you can buy your stock at $50 a share (3 for 1 split). Or, in researching your choices, you could find out that the president of the company you had chosen sold off most of his holdings last week and you decide to choose your second pick instead and wait and see what happens with company number one. Again, your library will have the recent issues available.

Be very careful to look at where the information you are reading is coming from. That is, is this being reported by a competitor who wants you to stop buying stock in the other company? Is the news release from a mutual fund company who wants to see the price of a particular stock drop so that they can afford to buy more for their portfolio? What kinds of information will you be looking for?

Let's say we found an article that said Chrysler idled the Belvidere IL plant due to slow sales of the Neon.

What does this mean? It does not mean anything by itself, but it gives you questions to ask yourself. If the company you are investing in is cutting back with eliminations, how will that effect the price of your stock (it could go down until things settle) and how will it affect your stock long term (cutting overhead could possibly mean higher profits)? Again, if a car manufacturing plant closes, will it effect another car manufacturer that you own stock in, or is this just due to the time of year when car sales are down anyway, or rather than interpreting it to mean that people are buying fewer cars, does it just mean that the market is changing and people are buying larger cars? In other words, these articles can create a question in your mind which may be easily answered in a future issue of The Wall Street Journal. But, in the meantime, and especially while you are learning about the market, you may want to take a wait and see position. When in doubt, don't do anything. Instead look for that company that you have no doubts about.

If while researching your favorites, you found some disturbing information, do you want to wait on that particular stock until things settle down or, because the company has such a strong history, do you want to wait for the price to drop a little because of this particular incident and buy in at a lower price? If your favorite pick is too high priced for you (or you are too impatient to save $25 a month until you have $150 to buy one share), you can continue saving or you can invest in a lower priced stock. We guarantee that you will feel very good knowing that you waited when that stock does split and you end up getting a great buy at $40 a share instead of $150. Or you can simply go to one of your other picks that has a more reasonable price of $40 a share.

There is nothing wrong with investing in your second or third pick first. If you have researched carefully and know that any of your three choices are good picks, start with the one that you can afford to start with. And if you truly cannot decide between three equally qualified stocks (we know some people have a hard time making decisions), try putting the three in a hat, close your eyes, and draw one out. Or subscribe to our monthly newsletter, "Common Sense Portfolio", or read "Top 50 Best Stock Investments".

Even after your initial investment, you may want to keep an eye on The Wall Street Journal's stock quotes page. This will tell you how your particular choice is doing today. However, remember that "a watched pot never boils". It can be frustrating to watch your stock going up and down every day. For most people it is much better to look at the stock quotes perhaps once a week or at least once a month. If you are the patient type of person, the Nightly Business Report on most PBS stations is very useful both for learning more about investing and for keeping up to date on only the important things concerning your own investment. There are many other financial shows on TV but this happens to be our favorite. If you become really devoted to investing, you will be watching CNBC all day!

The Wall Street Journal can be used for the same purpose. That is, use one of these on a daily or weekly or monthly basis (depending on how involved you want to be) to watch for important information such as when a split in your favorite stock is coming up. If you do hear or read about a forthcoming split, you might decide to quickly buy one share of that one **after it splits** to get started in your diversifying. We realize that suddenly jumping to another stock just because it drops to $40 a share is diversifying before you have collected 50 shares of your first investment. However, as you will see later in this chapter, there are very good reasons for buying just one share of a good stock at a good price while continuing to do your usual investing in your first company.

We need to point out here that all of this information can also be found online through Internet. Obviously, researching from your home is much easier, but be aware that some services do charge to enter their area. We cannot tell you in this book which ones will charge because this can and does change from week to week. But, if you have the capability, you will certainly want to check out each of your picks on Internet. If they are large enough companies (and if they are not, you should not be considering them), they will have an easy to find home page. That is, www.*name*.com. Here is where you can see their Annual and Quarterly Reports and any other information they want to give you. Notice, we said WANT to. When looking at any reports from the company, you must consider that they will only highlight the good news and try to hide the bad news from you. These large companies are usually very helpful if you send them online questions about their companies. Just remember that researching a particular company on the Internet is easy but you will not get the additional information about other companies you are interested in or any additional education in investment from the Internet. For more information and education, The Wall Street Journal will be the most useful.

You can also call any company you are interested in and ask them to mail you their most recent financial reports. To find the phone number for any business, look on that comany's Value Line page or ask your reference librarian for the phone number. Living in a free country, you can write a letter to the president or CEO of any company you want to. It could also prove interesting, and perhaps sway your choice, if you find that some executives are more willing to answer your questions than others are.

Also, if you find that you are becoming a little more interested in the stock market, our favorite daily television program is called Nightly Business Report. It is a half hour in which their aim seems to be to pack as much stock market information as is humanly possible into a half hour, so you have to listen carefully and develop a quick ear, but they do an excellent job of keeping you up to date on what is happening. And, while talking about television, if you are connected to a cable company, chances are one of your stations will have a ticker tape going across the bottom of the screen during the business day where you can watch your stock. Again, you will have to have fast eye sight to catch your particular stock. To find out what the call letters are for your stock, check the business section stock market listings of your daily paper or look beside the company name on the appropriate Value Line page.

You still have more information that you must research in order to make your money really grow. You will need to find out which companies offer automatic reinvestment plans.

**3. Reinvestment.** Do you have to choose only companies that have automatic dividend reinvestment plans? No, but it is a shame to waste an easy way to make money. What is reinvestment? Every stock, if it is doing well, will have a dividend or money that it pays to you for the use of your investment money, usually quarterly. Instead of getting this very tiny dollar amount sent to you, you can choose to have it automatically reinvested in the purchase of more stock for your portfolio **without paying a brokerage fee**. That is, any dividend that you have earned is automatically used to purchase more shares of the same stock. On each quarterly statement, you will see what the dividend was and how many more shares, or what part of a share, you just got for this reinvestment. With each statement, you can watch your financial portfolio growing, even if slowly.

In order to determine whether your picks offer reinvestment of dividends, you have to do one more step in researching, but a very easy step. Again look at the bottom of the appropriate Value Line page or simply use the companies phone number and call them. We can demonstrate by using General Electric as an example. Please note that it is unusual to have three splits within a 10 year period, but it is possible. The 10 year investment for GE looks like this:

1990  buy $100 worth of General Electric stock
1994  2-for-1 split
1997  2-for-1 split
2000  2-for-1 split
2000  $100 + splits + dividends = $11,026 (this does not include additional $25 a month for 10 years)

So your initial purchase of $100 became $11,026 without your lifting a finger due to splits and dividends. Your investment increased 110%, right? Wrong.

You also need to take into account the $25 you continued to invest every month for 10 years. This will bring your rate of increase per year to much more then 110%. By continuing to invest $25 every month in a strong company with a history of high growth that has automatic reinvestment of dividends and a good history of splits, you would end up with over $100,000 in that 10 year period. We hope that this example will encourage you to save that $25 every single month.

Here is another interesting example. If your grandfather bought 1 share of Coca-Cola (another very strong company with great growth) in 1919 for $40, you would now have over $191,000.00 (81 years but still very interesting). Again, this does not include investing $25 every month. However, it does include 2 world wars, 7 major depressions/recessions, and 1 major stock market crash. Is this usual for the stock market. No, it is not usual but there are other companies that have almost as good a history as General Electric and Coca-Cola.

The reinvestment option is a simple way to make your money grow by itself. It would be foolish for the small investor to put his money into a stock that does not have reinvestment of dividends. When you get older and are looking for income from your investment, you can cancel the reinvestment portion and have the dividends sent to you. But in order to get a dividend check for $500, you need to build your financial portfolio up enough to support that kind of dividend by using your $25 each month, by reinvesting the dividends, and by picking stock that has a history of splits.

Using the reinvestment option also saves you money. If you were to go through a broker and continue buying regularly until you have 50 shares, you will be paying whatever the current price is, high or low, plus paying that broker for purchasing additional shares for you. Very early in this book we mentioned the old adage, buy low and sell high. By using automatic reinvestment, you automatically buy low and sell high. As the price of your stock goes higher, your dividend will not be able to buy as much, so you automatically invest less when the price is higher. Then, when the price drops, your dividend automatically buys more stock at a lower price. And this is what everyone wants to do in the stock market - - invest more money when the market is low.

There is a second form of reinvestment that is **extremely important**.

**4. Direct Cash Purchase.** Before buying even one share of a company, call them to see if they have a Direct Cash Purchase Plan. This means that, after buying one share of stock, you can buy all future shares directly through the company and *they* pay the broker fees and expenses. Therefore, you are investing your money in your future and not in the stock brokers pocket. This part is what creates the huge growth for you. For instance, General Electric will accept a check for as little as $10 a year. So no matter how small your budget is, you too can participate in the stock market. Also ask them about direct withdrawal from your savings account. Some companies, such as GE, offer this and we know it is easier to save if you do not have to remember to mail in that check each month.

**5. Splits.** We have been talking a great deal about splits so let's define that word. A split is when a company needs more money to invest in order to grow, i.e. upgrading of equipment or research. But the Board of Directors should only vote for a split when the value of each share is high enough to warrant it (when the stock gets "pricey"), usually when it is over $100 and the average investor can no longer afford it (remember, buy low). At that point, the company will offer a split. It can be a 2-for-1 split, a 3-for-1 split, or even a 4-for-1 split. What does this mean for you?

If a stock splits 2-for-1, it means that you bought your first share for $50 and it has now grown to be worth $100 and tomorrow you will have 2 shares worth $50 each or $100 worth of stock. Didn't make any money, did you? So why are these splits so important? Because when a stock splits, it is a very strong encouragement for others to invest (remember, buy low), and as the demand increases for this great low-priced stock, the price tends to go back up again. Therefore, in a few months, those 2 shares that were worth $50 each will grow again to become 2 shares each worth $100. Your original $50 is now $100 without you spending one penny of your own money.

How do you find out about an upcoming split? The Wall Street Journal, your local newspaper's business page, and most television news shows will announce it. Now, if you want to spend as little time as possible on your investments, do _not_ read the next paragraph.

You see, it can be important for you to know about splits because if you suddenly come into a little extra money, immediately after that split would be the time to use it. That is, if you are getting money back from the IRS this year, or Aunt Sally always sends you a check for your birthday, or Uncle Peter died and left you everything, why not invest some or all of that extra income in your company IF the stock splits. If you are not interested in this little added bonus, then do not worry about it as your stock will continue to reinvest itself and split without you even noticing. If you do want to take advantage of the splits, you will need to spend that little bit of extra time watching the Nightly Business Report to know about it.

Another way to quickly increase your investment is to watch for the stock market to drop. A fact of life in a free society is business cycles. That is, the market will go up and down depending on who gets elected, what someone says, who died, etc. If you have a very safe stock you have invested in, and you see that stock following the rest of the market downward, and you have a little extra money, now would be a good time to buy up some more stock. Your reinvestment buys stock at the current price so that, when the price is high, it will take your reinvested dividends much longer to buy one whole share. If the market drops and your stock's price follows, you can get more stock at a much lower price. And remember that we are talking about very safe investments that will come back after a drop. Again using our Coca-Cola example, it not only survived the 1929 stock market crash, but within two years it had gained back everything it had lost. Remember, you are investing for the long term.

What is long term? We define long term for the stock market as a minimum of 5 years but preferably 10 years or longer. A research study by the University of Virginia showed that you can go all the way back to 1900 in the stock market and pull out any 5 year period you want. During that 5 year period, you would find that 3 years the market went up in value, 1 year it went down, and 1 year it stayed the same. In other words, just because of the factors built into our stock market, you have a 3 in 5 chance of making money in the market and a 4 in 5 chance of at least breaking even. If you use the market correctly!

**6. This is a joke!** We are adding this step just to show you what is possible. We are not recommending that you do this. We laid out one day's newspaper listing of the New York Stock Exchange. We then had our son, David, cover his eyes to pick out four companies and checked the selling price of each stock exactly one year before and the current closing price (for our purposes, we will not name them).

Stock #1 sold at 29 1/4 and closed that day at 26 3/8.

Stock #2 sold at 51 and closed that day at 58 1/4.

Stock #3 sold at 26 and closed that day at 26.

Stock #4 sold at 16 1/2 and closed that day at 14 7/8.


In other words, if he had used only this method and bought one share of each of these stocks exactly one year ago, he would have gained a total of 2 3/4 points total for these four shares or $2.75  for the year.  That does not seem like much, but the newspaper we used was during a very large two day drop in the stock market.  If we waited one more week and did the same thing, his four stocks would have shown an increase of $12.11.  Since he would have bought the shares for a total of $122.75, he would have had a 2% gain in one year.  And keep in mind that this was during a severe correction of the market and *by choosing at random.*  If we went back and showed the 10 year growth for those same four stocks, his overall gain was over 100%.  This is another example of why investing for the long term rather than for only one year is more profitable. This can be a fun thing to try on paper and maybe give you a little confidence in yourself when you make informed decisions rather than throwing darts and taking your chances.

We adamantly do **not** recommend this method but wanted to show you what can happen even when you do not first learn about the stock market and research your particular investments.

# V. TO MAKE THE INVESTMENT

## I'm Not A Jet-Setter; How Do I Go About This Investing?

In order to invest in the stock market, you must have a licensed broker invest your money. But sometimes you are not the one dealing with the broker (thus saving those fees) and it is important to make the distinction between different types of brokers.

Once you have decided to invest in a particular company, you want to check with them to see if you can buy the first share or shares directly through their broker. Yes, it may mean a little more money out of your pocket, but it all goes into your portfolio, not into broker fees. For instance, to buy just one share of Proctor & Gamble, you will need to go through a broker. But, if you are willing to buy $250 worth of stock to begin with, you can buy this directly through P&G thus avoiding dealing with a broker directly.

Obviously, this is the easiest way to buy stock and the best way to keep your money in your own pocket. However, if you want to invest in Coca-Cola, you must buy the first share or shares from a broker.

In the yellow pages you will find all of your local investment brokers plus some national ones with 800 numbers. Should you use a local broker? Well, do you believe in supporting your local businesses? Do you want to deal with a live person or just a voice on the phone? You need to answer these two questions yourself. Also, you need to know that a regular broker will charge a high fee and sometimes have additional fees that they may not tell you about over the phone when you call to check out costs. Yes, you do get something for this higher fee. You will be given the brokers learned advice on your investments, and he will do the research for you, but he will not give you any guarantee that your money will grow or even that it will not decrease.

But you have to go through a broker so we always use **discount brokers**. A discount broker will take your order and make the purchase, period. No advice, no extra information. We believe this is the way to go because making decisions concerning your money should be your responsibility. In fact, if you decide to go with a regular broker and do as he tells you, you have taken the responsibility to make that decision and, therefore, have only yourself to blame for paying those higher fees.

Our method uses only discount brokers. In return for taking responsibility and making your investment decisions, you get much lower fees.

Quick & Reilly is a nationally known brokerage that does offer to do one share purchases but check out others in your area also. You will find that their fees do vary a great deal depending on how much they want your business. Whoever you choose must be **listed** with the New York Stock Exchange. Please be aware that brokers have a tendency to give the small investor a difficult time. Obviously, they want you to invest more and will try to talk you into spending more money any way they can.

Now let's use an average discount broker's fee of $35. This will be the amount they will charge you to make a minimum purchase. But remember that this is a one-time fee for your first purchase. After you get that first share, your dividends will reinvest without paying a brokerage fee AND each month or quarter you will invest that $25-a-month directly in the company you bought without any more broker's fees. Your statement will have a form that you can send back in with your check to buy more stock directly through the company without going through your discount broker. Continuing to invest that $25 each and every month is what will give you the huge growth that we are looking for.

Many people ask us about doing transactions **online**. We cannot recommend this for three reasons. One, anyone can create a website pretending to be a broker, collect your fees and checks for one month, and then close their doors. Please only deal with well-known brokerages. Two, transactions, particularly on busy market days, are very slow. Many of the best known online brokerages have had delays of over two days in actually doing your transaction. Thus there can be a big difference between what price you thought you were buying the stock for and what price you actually bought the stock for. Three, and most important, at this time there is no online broker that will allow you to have your stock in your own name. Thus they keep control of your stock and will charge you monthly expenses for this "service".

## VI.  TRACKING YOUR INVESTMENTS

### What If I Don't Want To Spend My Time Doing Bookkeeping?

Then don't!  Tracking your investments can be fun and exciting or it can be very boring and depressing.  Therefore, we suggest that you do minimal tracking but enough to satisfy Uncle Sam and enough to show you what you are accomplishing.

There are a lot of specialized software packages you can buy to keep track of your finances on your computer and, if you really love playing with your computer, this could work for you.  But all that is really necessary is to have a manila file folder that is kept in a safe location (and one where you will not forget what you did with it).  Every time something arrives in the mail from the company you bought, put it into that folder - - even if you don't bother to open it and read it!  You will need this information when you decide to sell some stock.

If you become very interested in investing, you may want to keep closer track of your investments either on the computer or in a notebook. However, we believe in doing things in a simple manner and we also know that, if you decide to follow your investments on a daily basis, you can go insane! The market goes up and down continually. We do not want you to panic when you see your stock going through a downward trend and sell it off only to discover that, if you had kept it long-term as we suggest, the price would go back up again and make you even more of a profit.

What this all boils down to is our philosophy of investing for the long term.

> **Invest for the long term because, if you have chosen wisely, the market will correct itself and you will make even higher profits then you would by selling at the first sign of danger.**

There will be times to **sell**. Specifically, when you have reached one of your goals such as the down payment on your new home. But even then, you do not sell immediately. Barring a terrible disaster to you or your family, you will have plenty of time to decide exactly when to sell. This time should be used to research the market again. Find out how your company is doing, is there a split coming up that you would not want to miss, has the market recently been going down and effecting the value of your stock, or has it been going up and looks like it will continue to go up?  Clearly, you want to get the most for your money.  So plan ahead when you need to sell some of your stock.

When you decide to **sell** some stock, the first thing you **must** do is call the company's investor services and ask if they are doing a **buy-back**.  Many companies have a buy-back program wherein they want to retire outstanding shares that have been issued to the public.  That is, they have excess cash and want to invest it to make more money for their company.  If they have a good strong company (the kind that we are looking to invest in) that is where they will invest.  They buy-back shares in their own company knowing that, when they need more cash for further expansion or whatever, they can re-sell those shares at a higher price then they bought them for.  A buy-back also help you because, in order to entice you into selling back those shares, they will offer a premium price, usually 25 cents to 50 cents a share more then the current market value.  Plus, they pay the broker transaction fee.

However, if you want to sell some shares and the company is not doing a buy-back, you will have no choice but to go to a discount broker to sell those shares.  Again, check with the different brokers because their transaction fees will vary.

## VII.  EASY AND SAFE INVESTING


### You Don't Have To Be Rich To Become Rich

If you follow this method of investing, you will never have to spend hours worrying about your investments.  By selecting large companies with a good 5 year (preferably a 10 year) track record of gains including splits, by immediately signing up for their reinvestment program, and by adding your $25 every single month, your portfolio will grow quickly.  Make your money work for you instead of you working for your money.

Can you become rich on $25 a month?  Well, we are firm believers that the term rich is relative.  For some people, just having a retirement income of $1,000 a month will suffice.  For others, only several million dollars will do.  Either way, the answer to the question is yes, you can become rich on your investments.  However, the best way to do that is to enlarge your investments.  You may be able to afford only $5 a month right now, but what about next year?  Will you get a raise and be able to make it $10 a month?  What about 10 years down the road?  Will you be able to afford $200 a month?  All it takes is a little of your time to go over your budget each new year and decide what you want to accomplish for the coming year.  And, while you are at it, look at the previous year and see if you carried through on what you wanted to accomplish.  It does not matter if you did not do as well as you had hoped to do - - just start over again tomorrow.

Remember to relax and enjoy your investing.  You may actually find that it is fun to become involved in what a major corporation is doing.  And it is definitely fun to watch your money growing.  It could even lead to a new career for you.  You might even enjoy attending an annual share holders meeting.  Some companies even provide their share holders with extra little perks.

Perks are little extras that you may get as a share holder.  For instance, Hershey has been known to give out gift boxes or samples of their newest products.  And keep in mind that if you have friends or relatives that live in Atlanta and you buy stock in Coca-Cola which is based in Atlanta, you should plan your get-togethers around the annual share holders meeting.  By attending the meeting, your travel expenses are tax deductible as a business expense.  This is another good reason to open up any mail from your investment to see where the annual meeting will take place. Maybe next year it will be in Hawaii.

A fact of life is that the only way to succeed when you start your own business is to work long hours seven days a week and never give up. Even if that business fails, figure out what went wrong and try again. In other words, there is one thing we can promise you - - you can only succeed at anything by using persistence. When you invest in the stock market, life gets easier in that you only have to persist when it comes to making that additional $25 investment each and every month.

You do not have to be a genius to accomplish what you want in life and have investments that will take care of you. You just have to spend a little time and never give up. You might decide to stop using our method and try a riskier method hoping to increase your gains. Or you might decide to just keep your money in a savings account. But whatever you do, do not give up saving for your future. If Henry Ford had given up, not only would he have poor grandchildren, but where would the economy of this country be without that transportation? You will be effecting our economy also, to a greater or lesser extent than Ford, but you will be effecting it.

The thing that people do in their lives that causes the most unhappiness is **putting it off till tomorrow**. This is true of every aspect of your life.  We have written extensively about this in Bobbie's other books, but it is just as true for your financial life.  You may be reading this sentence right now and thinking "next month I'll start that".  Whenever you put something off, the chances of ever doing it drop dramatically.  So start right now by making the list of essential and non-essential investment possibilities. Tomorrow go to the library and do the research. The next day, call that company to see if you can invest directly through them or if you must go through a broker.  Then send in that check or call that broker and start building your future.

Only **you** can start building your financial portfolio (unless you suddenly inherit a great deal of money or you win the lottery).  And teach your children how to invest for their future. Having the opportunity to invest your own money is a privilege that most people in this world do not have.  We Americans have that privilege.  Use this opportunity for yourself.

## Books by Bobbie and Eric Christensen

*Building Your Debt-Free Life*  ($14.95)

*Top 50 Best Stock Investments*  ($24.95)

*Building Your Financial Portfolio On $25 A Month (Or Less)*  ($14.95)

*Adding To Your Financial Portfolio* ($14.95)

## Books by Bobbie Christensen

*Building Your Dream Life: Career, Sex & Leisure* ($14.95)

*Getting A Free Education: The Key To Your Dream Job* ($11.95)

*Self-Publishing & Marketing Your Book (on a shoe-string budget)*  ($10.00)

*All books add $1.50 for shipping and handling.

## Newsletters

*Common Sense Portfolio*  ($25.00 for 1 year, $45.00 for 2 years, $21.00 for email version)

*American Self-Publisher*  (included with membership for $45.00 per year)

**To order, call 1-800-929-7889** (Mastercard & Visa accepted)
or mail check or money order to:
Effective Living Publishing, POBox 232233, Sacramento, CA 95823
or visit:
www.BooksAmerica.com (investing and self-help)

Prices guaranteed through 12/00

# BIBLIOGRAPHY

Heatter, Justin. The Small Investors Guide To Large Profits In The Stock Market. Charles Scribner's Sons, NY, 1983.

Kehrer, Daniel. 12 Steps to a Worry-Free Retirement. Random House, NY, 1995.

Lehmann, Michael B. Using The Wall Street Journal. Business One Irwin, IL, 1993.

O'Neil, William J. How To Make Money In Stocks. McGraw-Hill, Inc., NY, 1995.

Porter, Sylvia. Your Finances in the 1990's. Prentice Hall Press, NY, 1990.

Quinn, Jane Bryant. Making the Most of Your Money. Simon & Schuster, NY, 1991.

Siegel, Jeremy J. and Irwin, Richard D. Stocks For The Long Run. Irwin, Inc., NY, 1994.

Spitz, William T. Get Rich Slowly. MacMillan, NY, 1992.

Walden, Gene. The 100 Best Stocks To Own In America. Longman Financial Services Publishing, 1989.

Whitaker, Leslie. The Beardstown Ladies' Common-Sense Investent Guide. Hyperion, NY, 1994.

Whitney, Russ. Building Wealth. Simon & Schuster, NY, 1994.